D1602974

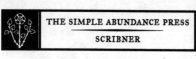

THE SIMPLE ABUNDANCE PRESS

SCRIBNER

Instructions
for Your Discontent

How Bad Times Can Make Life Better

Barrie Dolnick

<small>WITH A FOREWORD BY</small>
Sarah Ban Breathnach

THE SIMPLE ABUNDANCE PRESS
SCRIBNER

NEW YORK   LONDON   TORONTO   SYDNEY   SINGAPORE

THE SIMPLE ABUNDANCE PRESS
SCRIBNER

1230 Avenue of the Americas
New York, NY 10020

For information regarding special discounts for bulk purchases
please contact Simon & Schuster Special Sales at 1-800-456-6798
or business@simonandschuster.com

DESIGNED BY ERICH HOBBING

Text set in Palatino

Manufactured in the United States of America

1   3   5   7   9   10   8   6   4   2

Library of Congress Cataloging-in-Publication Data
Dolnick, Barrie.
Instructions for your discontent: how bad times can make life better/Barrie Dolnick.
p. cm.
1. Change (Psychology) 2. Discontent. I. Title.
BF637.C4D65 2003
158.1—dc21
2003041567

ISBN 0-7432-1442-0

For my mom,
Sandy Dolnick, my first Instructor

Contents

Contents

The Final Word ☺

Instructions
for Your Discontent

Foreword

by Sarah Ban Breathnach

Two years ago I was grumbling to my wise and witty friend Barrie Dolnick about something or other. She listened attentively and with great affection, then told me to buck up and start following my own advice: become grateful that I was feeling so ornery, restless, and miserable because it meant Divine Discontent was stirring things up in my soul and change was on the way. Since I welcome change the way a concrete wall looks forward to the wrecking ball, this was not exactly what I wanted to hear. And what was I supposed to do in the meantime? "Funny you should ask," she replied with a wry grin. She was writing a manual called *Instructions for Your Discontent.* I begged her to let me start reading her unfinished manuscript, and with Barrie's hallmark generosity of spirit she did. I finished her first few chapters in one sitting, then started over again. Those original dog-eared pages have become the book you now hold in your hands.

If ever there were a quintessential self-help book (as in help yourself back to sanity and serenity, word by word), this one is it. Often when we're going down for the third, fourth, or fifth time with any difficult, discouraging, and recurring situation in our life (and getting nowhere), it's time to stop holding fast to beliefs that don't work anymore. We need an attitude adjustment as powerful and as transformative as reconsidering discontent a blessing, not a curse. As the English historian Dame Cicely Veronica Wedgwood points out, "Discontent and disorder [are] signs of energy and hope, not of despair." It just doesn't feel that way when we're mired in our misery. But help is here.

It's been my good fortune to have Barrie Dolnick act as a loving, compassionate, and savvy guide during my own magical, mystical mystery tour, known as Life, and it gives me great pleasure to introduce you to each other. Quite frankly, I believe *Instructions for Your Discontent* is a gift of grace (and may all the world's cynics be the first in line to surrender their self-imposed shackles of skepticism and smirks). As for the rest of you, those who waver daily between the ebb and flow of faith and doubt, get comfy and play with the idea that the same thinking that keeps you a grimacing malcontent isn't the one that's going to help you start grinning again. But pondering and then following Barrie Dolnick's provocative and persuasive suggestions will. At the very least, I think you'll discover, in the warmth, wit, and wisdom of this profound and sassy book, a writer and chum who really does understand what it's like to wake up every morning and not want to get out of bed. Barrie's enthusiasm for change is contagious and comforting; actually reading this book in bed with a cup of something warm is soothing and therapeutic!

While you might think you're only perusing a book called *Instructions for Your Discontent*, I suspect you'll discover, as I did, nothing less than a practical, creative, spiritual, and smile-inducing manual on how to spin straw into gold. And that's certainly worth a read.

Preface

Principles of the Instructions

What you are about to encounter is a little strange. You're just going to have to get over that. These Instructions work. I can attest to it. That said, if the discontent we encounter together in this book isn't suitable for these Instructions, you'll be encouraged to seek help elsewhere. I always enjoyed those Dear Abby columns where she evenly and firmly indicated that the concerned letter writer should seek professional help. If your brand of discontent is outside my experience, you're going to know it.

Discontent is a truly universal experience: you're going to see many of your friends, family, and colleagues in this book. But you're the only one who can follow these Instructions. You can't fix other people. You can only fix yourself. Apply these Instructions liberally to your life and you will, by example and by healing, help others. But that's as far as it goes.

The tenets in this book aren't founded on "what's right" but on finding "what's the right thing for you." One person's ambrosia is another person's arsenic. You're the only one who can call the shots in your life. It's your free will, which is the most difficult and the most blessed thing about it. Yet you may be tempted to judge someone else's choices or way of life. When your attention starts to wander in someone else's direction and you feel the urge to utter "Ugh" or point out the error of his ways, resist! You are here to explore your own reality, not to judge others. You're here by the grace of God (or whatever the Great Energy may be to you) and no one appointed you (or me) keeper of the Right Way. If people around you seem to be going astray, let them—as long as they don't harm anyone else. If no one is hurt (I mean gravely hurt) by

3

another's choices, you have no reason to interfere. This is what's known as the *harm-none principle*.

Some of these Instructions require action on your part. Most of them require you to reevaluate your beliefs. In many ways, your beliefs about the way the world works can keep you from finding serenity and happiness. You will be challenged to look into what you have accepted to be "right" about the world. This isn't to say that you're wrong, but the "Re-Beliefs" in this book can enhance your vision, expand your scope, and broaden hope and healing.

Discontent can't be contained or outlined to fit your agenda or your convenience. It appears in your life in its own time and place and pops up in almost every area you can imagine. For that reason, this book is organized based on the most commonly expressed discontents to the less expressed but certainly no less important.

Discontent has layers, like an onion. The outer layers are typically the problems that we're more willing to share with others. We can all gripe about money—that's perfectly acceptable. We can complain about other people, too. That's not too far from the surface. Money and love are the two most pervasive forms of discontent. The inner layers are more personal and less commonly articulated. These are personal issues that include self-esteem, time management, anger, and your inner spiritual life. For this book, we'll work from the outside in, but you can go wherever you need the Instruction. Be sure to read the first two chapters before you get started.

You're going to enjoy examining your discontent, and moreover, you're going to love being happy again.

Discontent: The Initiation

Restlessness is your first clue.

Discontent can creep into your life, making you feel uncomfortable, as if sitting too long in a cramped space. Initially, discontent can make you grumpy and coax you into a bad mood. Later, as discontent settles more permanently into your routine (I hate my job, I'm so lonely, I can't get ahead), you feel much more sour about your life and your future. Discontent is heavy. It dampens your spirit and whites out your hope. Discontent can make you feel sluggish, dissociated, disinterested, even disabled. Discontent starts with a single facet of your life, but left unchecked, it can eventually overwhelm your entire life.

This isn't depression—you are functioning pretty well and you're not sad—but you're definitely not happy either. You just can't seem to get comfortable.

Discontent comes in many guises and for all occasions. It's epidemic and unique, mutable and fixed, relentless and forgiving. Discontent appears to be an enemy of all that is good in your life, and when it leaves, you're grateful—not only for finally feeling good again, but because you feel even better than you did before. You're more solid and more confident. Now you're able to create even more happiness.

Discontent strips you to your most vulnerable to reveal to you your strength. It wrestles you to the ground until you yell "Uncle!" and surrender to its grasp.

No matter how happy you think you are, if you're getting fidgety, you're coming down with a case of discontent. Here are some common symptoms.

Dragging out of bed every morning.
Increased cravings for coffee, sugar, binge foods, or alcohol.

Decreased interest in pleasures.
Too much TV.
Putting on weight.
Laughing less—especially at yourself.
Calling all glasses "half-empty."
Looking for approval from anyone who can give it.
Often using the term "It's not fair."
Putting yourself down.
Putting others down.
Constantly being asked "What's wrong?"
Feeling overlooked, unappreciated.
Feeling tired even when you're rested.
Feeling as if your life is in someone else's hands.
Lying because you're afraid that truth isn't good enough.
Being suspicious of others.
Losing your temper.

Listen to the rumbles beneath your daily life. As you face your unique race against time, tasks, and the demands of a job and family and your life, take a moment to pay attention to your underlying feelings. If you do, you may notice that discontent is often there, growling from a corner of your psyche through the peaceful moments. It may emerge during a traffic jam, or after a phone call from a friend. It may jab at you during unguarded, undistracted moments so that in a split second your composure, your peace of mind, and your mood all deteriorate.

I'm a perfect example. While I have most of what I've always wanted in life—my husband, my child, work I love, and the health of my loved ones—I'm still prone to ignoring the claws of discontent. I like to keep things moving. I want to be a supportive partner and an attentive, good mother. I want to continue to write and speak and evolve in my work. But when I find myself wishing I lived within the easy parameters of a TV sitcom where problems get solved in thirty minutes, or when I start envying the characters who live on Birdwell Island in my daughter's favorite Clifford cartoon, I know that discontent has come to visit. I notice myself in a fantasy of other perfect worlds when all I have to work with is right in front of me. I know that discontent is not an omen of bad times, but I also know it takes work and energy to deal with it. And it doesn't go away in thirty minutes of snappy dialogue.

Part of me wants to be discontented all the time. This bizarre urge is no doubt born from two distinct idiosyncrasies. The first is my peasant within who thinks that the evil eye won't fall on me if I don't smile. That's a fake-out, a way to affect unhappiness in order to avoid it. The second is slightly more complex. Discontent is not a bad thing. In fact, the fruits of discontent are generally sweet, and you will most likely "fix" your discontent by bettering yourself or your circumstances. Discontent forces you to make changes in your life to rediscover contentment or happiness. This is why I almost want to be in some evolving discontent; that way I know my life is going to improve, that the "dis" will disappear and leave me contented.

Thank goodness for discontent. Without it, I'd never have gotten off that couch in Wisconsin and moved out into the world, where adventure, love, opportunity, change, and other spicy moments awaited me. Thank goodness for feeling lousy, bored, angry, ignored, put down, overlooked, and just about every other offense one can feel from the world. Without those unpleasant prods, I wouldn't have found or defined my passion and my compassion, my truth and my humor, my laziness and my ambition.

My experiences with discontent have spurred me to become an expert in how to get happy again or, at least, how not to be unhappy.

During my thirteen years with Madison Avenue ad agencies, I learned how to evaluate the desires, aspirations, wants, and needs of all different kinds of people. (The best marketing strategies will diagnose a source of consumer discontent and offer a compelling solution—for a price.) On a less pragmatic level, I compounded my understanding of discontent with fifteen years of study in the areas of astrology, meditation, intuitive and psychic powers, and alternative beliefs and philosophies. When I left advertising to write books, I also started a consulting business that helps clients identify and pursue career goals, navigate choices, and keep up with the changing marketplace. I use astrology, tarot cards, and metaphysical information to help my clients dissolve their discontent and open to their best possible futures.

Just as powerful in my training, though, are my personal experiences with discontent—and I'll share many of them with you. I am an Instructor, but I'm also attending continuing-education classes in life.

That is true for you, too. Discontent will be the driving force for most changes in your life. And it should be. That's why these Instructions will be handy.

The Creative State of Discontent

Discontent can be a blessing. It is an intensely creative state that nags and pokes you to get yourself going and accomplish what you really want in life.

I regard almost my entire career in advertising as one of my most flagrant and long-term discontents. At the outset, I was grateful to have found my first job at a prestigious company. I realized quickly, though, that I didn't give a nut for the toilet cleaner I was to help sell, or for the cheap perfume I was to help create. I had no authentic enthusiasm for my work. On top of that, I had to learn and play the game of managerial politics and adhere to corporate-soldier rules. I felt like an actress, dressing for the role of "get-ahead" executive while harboring an eye-rolling scofflaw in my suit.

I soon realized that I despised what I was doing and for whom I was doing it, and that I was one Crabby Appleton. Add up thirteen years of doing it, and I was a veritable bitch in pumps.

I'm still friendly with some of the people I knew in my advertising career, many of whom are happily and effectively marketing products and services. They tease me once in a while about how completely impossible I was back then, and we laugh over the old stories we share. And in retrospect, I know I am blessed to have had every moment of that experience. Being in advertising and greatly discontented gave me my first taste of real-life issues, situations, and conflicts. Everyone had his own agenda. A few people actually cared about the work, but most were either jockeying for power or trying to avoid responsibility. Pass the buck and make a buck. Through working with difficult people, I learned patience and how to make myself heard. From making mistakes, I learned how to take blame and how to dissolve useless finger-pointing. I also tried to learn to keep my mouth shut, which is something I continue to struggle with. Most important, though, I learned to hone my intuition and to trust my feelings rather than rationalize and try to go with the group's way of thinking. I learned so much more than just how to sell soap. And I got frustrated enough to leave the business to do something I love.

I harbor enormous compassion for people in that creative state called discontent, and I hold extraordinary certainty that they—and we—will find a way out of it.

Surrendering Is the First Fight

I recall when I attended the University of Massachusetts in Amherst. I was a freshman, studying "Pre-Business" (that's a whole other discontent story), and living on my own away from Wisconsin for the first time. I had been determined to fly from my Midwestern cocoon and attend college in the East. I arrived with gusto, in search of a studious yet *Love Story*–worthy year of deep experiences.

I got nothing like it. I lived in an unromantic high-rise dormitory. My roommate was never there and I was lonely. While my high school friends enjoyed themselves at the University of Wisconsin and went through rush, I tried desperately to find spirit in a lackluster football team. It wasn't that I liked football, but that's what you were supposed to do in college, I thought, and I worked on posing as best I could as Ali MacGraw's Jennie, studious yet impossibly good-looking in a natural sort of way. I failed on all fronts. Pretentious behavior is a great symptom of discontent. I wasn't happy because I was trying to force an experience that for me wasn't authentic, organic, or true. But I tried: no way was I going to regret coming here. I took classes at Amherst College; I went to lectures at Smith. I stopped short of wearing knee socks and plaid skirts, but the thought crossed my mind. I hated it all. Reading the letters I received from my high school buddies (this was before e-mail) filled me with longing and envy. What was I missing? Was I really missing anything? Maybe they were just embellishing their good times.

I tried to keep my chin up, but eventually I succumbed to teary phone calls home. When my father suggested I transfer back to the University of Wisconsin, I muttered a few weak protests and then admitted the truth: I was unhappy, I had made a poor choice. I was full of discontent.

This is the critical point in dismantling discontent. You don't have to cry (but it's common) and you don't have to see a therapist or an astrologer (but that can be helpful, too). You only have to admit how you feel. That final breaking point when you confess that you're not okay is usually "turnaround" time. Discontent stops pressuring you.

Liberation comes next, and that requires invoking your own energy to break out of those limitations. Once I gave myself permission to leave U-Mass, I dealt with my pride, which had kept me from ever considering a change of school, and I applied for a transfer.

I remember, back in my senior year of high school, announcing to my friends, "I just wouldn't fit in at a Big Ten school. I could never go there." A statement like that is practically the kiss of death when it comes to discontent. If you litter your sentences with "I could never" or "I'm just not that type," you can pretty much be sure that eventually you'll have to do it. And that's a hard surrender to face.

My former astrology teacher and close friend Susan Strong always reminds me (when I'm steeping in some new discontent), *"You get what you resist."* It's totally true. Whatever you absolutely refuse to consider at the outset of your discontent is probably going to take center stage. So dance with your monsters. Welcome the pain. The critical point of shifting out of discontent is admission, but the only way to liberate yourself is by transition: taking an active role and doing something about it. It doesn't sound so good, but it works.

Knowing you're not in good shape is great, but you'll stay there or worsen if you don't take action. Inaction at the critical point results in depression.

No Denying It

Discontent is not something you should deny any more than you would deny a lump under your arm. For a physical problem, such as a lump, human nature would scare up a load of reasons why it's probably nothing, but you would still be encouraged (by your friends if not your conscience) to have it examined, diagnosed, and dealt with. Discontent isn't so pressing or ominous, and you can't go and have it "cured," but you can be your own doctor, in a way, and at least delve into self-diagnosis.

You can, and probably will, try to ignore the ugly feelings associated with discontent for some time. When you can't talk yourself out of your uneasiness anymore, you'll have two choices: conscious denial or active acceptance. Conscious denial will eventually land you somewhere among three conditions: dysfunctional living, addiction, or depression. Usually, you get a combination platter.

Nonaction

Some people choose nonaction. They just get angrier inside but never let it out; they refuse to do anything at all to help themselves. I've seen it with passive-aggressive people. It's irritating to those who love them, and after a while, these folks are seriously unlovable.

Nonaction also takes the form of anesthesia, ways to deaden the mind, body, emotions, and spirit instead of feel the pain of discontent. There are many ways to anesthetize. Most obvious is self-medication, such as drinking or popping recreational drugs or binge eating, until you don't notice that you're, like, um, addicted. It's a way of numbing your feelings, but the more you numb, the harder your feelings fight to come to the surface, so the more you need to cover them up. It's a vicious cycle that ends up harming your body.

You can also take your discontent out on everyone around you. But like those passive-aggressive types, sooner or later you won't have a lot of people to pick on. This is where I'm most skilled. Until I worked on myself—which in many ways was simply about knowing myself—I was a blamer, a criticizer, a coveter. And I was very much at home in my discontent.

Some people anesthetize themselves with so-called spiritual pursuits, such as dropping out of their relationships, work, or family life to follow a cult or a guru. It's a way of handing over your life to someone else's power, so that even if you're discontented, that choice has been made for you in the name of God. You don't have to take responsibility, just do what you're told. This is a sad cop-out. You don't even get to live your life's potential when you hand your free will to someone else.

"Dysfunctions" can play out in thousands of ways. The core of each, however, is pretty common: putting others' needs before your own. Dysfunctional living is also clearly the result of some contained discontent; dysfunction typically relies on keeping secrets, not telling the truth, indirect communication, and other unhealthy, inauthentic daily behavior. It takes a lot of work to keep up the status quo when your life has an unnatural rhythm or lacks harmony. In many situations where we convince ourselves that the expedient or easy thing to do is also something that makes others happy (isn't that a good deed?), these decisions come back to bite us with discontent.

Basically, you have to be honest and admit that you're experiencing discontent. Then you act on it so you can be happy again. In this book I'm going to open your eyes to various roads you can take, but I can't make you go there. You have to do that on your own.

Instructions in a Nutshell

Confront discontent. (Surrender!)
Appreciate its source.
Take action (Instructions).
Laugh again.

The Initiation

You can be brilliant, accomplished, prepare a gourmet meal, and raise healthy, well-adjusted children and *still* fall into discontent. After all, you're still human, vulnerable, and evolving.

Custom-Fit Discontent

Your discontent is different from your neighbor's.

Discontent mutates its way through the population like a virus that adapts to each person's emotional and spiritual immune system. If you're prone to dramatics, your discontent will probably be worn on the outside of your skin so that everyone knows about it. If you're more private, you'll hide it under layers of dignity and calm. Most of us are somewhere in between, baring our anxiety to trusted friends but maintaining a cool facade with others.

Discontent isn't an outside situation. It's always internal. You can't share it or let someone try it on to see how it fits. My brand of discontent feels like a black hole in my belly, an uneasy density that can't be balanced or soothed. It's often expressed in anger. My friend Julia's discontent is a disquiet, a thin veil of anxiety that creates an inaccessible, soft-focused world; it's hard for her to connect to the outside. She doesn't speak about it. Cherry, another close friend, keeps her discontent to the side until she can't deny it and then is overwhelmed by her own body—headaches, negative thoughts, instant indigestion. My mother-in-law, a deeply loving woman, feels heavy in her heart when she's steeped in discontent. She feels uncomfortable and worried and can't find a peaceful moment. My husband is different. He talks about being uncomfortable in his skin and constantly fidgets to soothe his malaise.

Your discontent is contained within you exactly the way it's supposed to be. Whether it's in your body, your mind, your heart, or your energy level, it's an insidious presence demanding attention.

The Privilege of Discontent

You'd think that money and power fend off discontent, but they're more like magnets. You don't feel discontent when you're worried about keeping a roof over your head, or when you have some terrible illness or your family is in dire circumstances. If you're in a "state of emergency," you're fully vested in a justifiable survival anxiety. You don't need to examine it, just do what you have to do to make it go away. Discontent is a luxury afforded to those of us who live in relative peace, with plenty of food and no major risks to our health or home. Less fortunate souls living in famine, poverty, deprivation, war, despotism, don't have the luxury of discontent. They just want to be able to live.

Discontent is an integral part of the process of fulfillment, and when you have taken care of your survival and security, you will have a lot of time to think about your fulfillment.

Discontent is a privilege.

Once you're no longer concerned with finding shelter, food, and safety, you are wide open to some prods of discontent. It's my theory that the more money you have, the more acute your needs are. This is because we tend to believe the myth that money can buy just about anything. Yet no amount of dough is going to make you feel good about yourself. It can patch you up with a good-looking mate and perhaps make people treat you with respect (but still be able to turn away and snigger). Yet having money can give you a false sense of being able to appease your discontent because you have more options: a big home, plastic surgery, private lessons (in whatever you want), lavish parties, luxury vacations.

Ultimately, the only cure for discontent, with or without money, is the ability to face it and work with it. You may be able to buy yourself a good therapist, but you still have to do the work yourself.

Those of you who don't have fat billfolds, don't be jealous: you'll get to the root of your discontent faster because you won't have so much money to blow on avoiding it.

I see a lot of discontent. I've seen it in teenagers (they could market it as a bestselling fashion), young adults, and grown-up men and women with lionhearted careers and families who exude perfection. Discontent is a great leveler that takes every one of us back to our basic needs, hopes, and wishes. There is no obstruction in life worse than our own unhappiness.

In most cases when I'm asked for help, I can give it. In a few instances, however, I'm not as effective, and that's when fear has eclipsed hope.

A few years ago, a successful businessman came to see me and told me about his life. He was stymied by his discontent, but he wouldn't admit that much of anything was wrong. His business had hit a rough patch, but he was philosophical about business cycles. He had a great relationship with his daughter and was on reasonably good terms with his ex-wife. He had his health. I asked about his love life and he stated with unconvincing certainty that he wasn't interested in falling in love. He claimed he liked dating casually and that was enough. I probed a little, as one does in front of a false wall, and soon he admitted that his marriage had been a great love that had turned sour, bitter, and horrible. He didn't want to be in that situation again. He was afraid of being emotionally devastated and liked having the upper hand in lighter relationships.

Yet I could sense a longing for love.

I had no way to help him because he was too afraid to admit that he wanted to find a love relationship. I did offer advice about opening up to deeper connections, but he shrugged it off. I felt helpless in the face of his fear. He didn't want to be vulnerable, and his fear of his vulnerability made it impossible for him even to try to open up. He had a gaping need to be in love and refused even to try. He closed the door on hope and thus shut out happiness.

I write this book in hopes that this man and people like him will understand that they can dare to hope again. They can move beyond their isolation in discontent. They are not alone; we all go through it. Like us, they can feel again; not just feel bad, but feel better than ever.

Seven Familiar Signs of Discontent
(aka the Seven Deadly Sins)

Discontent can creep up on us in the form of bad habits or attitudes. You don't necessarily recognize the symptoms right away, but you slowly realize that you're indulging yourself in something you consider "bad." You can often self-diagnose with our old friends, the Seven Deadly Sins. Over time, they might all make an appearance. Here, I speak from personal experience.

I've noticed that I'm prone to gluttony by overindulging in chocolate, French fries, grilled-cheese sandwiches, whatever I crave when I'm feeling down. If I'm teetering on the brink of discontent, one stressful phone call that touches my self-esteem or insecurity can catapult me into the kitchen to rummage through my chocolate reserves. I will still be on the cordless phone as I unwrap an old chocolate bar or, at my lowest, crack open some chocolate chips or cookie dough. Discontent throws me off my diet; it brings gluttonous behavior to the surface. I will eventually find I've gained weight, and that brings about yet another sin, yet another symptom of discontent: vanity. The minute I've gained a few pounds, my self-esteem plummets and I get needy. Tell me I'm smart, pretty, fun, loving—anything nice—then tell me again. I need that reassurance. Don't tell anyone that I'm this way, though, because I'll deny it outright. After all, I have my pride.

I just hate it when I see other people managing to keep their weight down and I'm doing time at the Whitman's Sampler. Why can't I look like that? I want everyone to be fat like me or at least, if they're skinny, to be miserable. This qualifies as envy.

What I need is to feel good about myself. I need to be appreciated for all of me! That's why, when I saw those amazing Jimmy Choo shoes in the window, I had to buy them. Of course, all I really needed was a little pick-me-up, a little indulgence to make me feel better. And I do! And since I have those darling shoes, I probably need a nice new outfit to show them off. It's always nice to treat yourself, right? I saw this great skirt and jacket in the window at

Armani, and I positively lusted after it. So I bought it. That's it. I've satisfied my desires. No more lusting for more.

Now that I've accepted myself with my fuller figure, I do find myself without so much to wear, though. So I've been shopping, replacing things I need. It's no big deal. My friend got this great handbag in an Internet auction and I was so jazzed by it (another form of discontent peeks in here—using age-inappropriate slang!), I did it myself. Now I can't stop. It's amazing the stuff you can buy. Not that I need it all, but it's so much fun! Am I being just a tad greedy?

Of course, when my credit card bills arrive, I am furious. I was charged so much interest! I'm really mad. I accidentally yelled at my neighbor when he dropped off one of my bills the mailman had misdelivered to him. I can't believe he called me a hothead. I'm certainly not temperamental—or defensive. I don't know what he's talking about. I'm not so angry. Am I?

Now that I've got to cool off in the shopping department, I've realized that I'm just tired. I need to rest. I've got to take better care of myself. So I'm not going to the gym just now. And I'm not going to put too much pressure on myself at work. I've got this great book about the ten ways to live life in its simplest form, and I'm going to read it and make sure that I'm operating in a spiritual way. On my couch. No need to exert any effort. Just be. Just breathe. I'll get to all those chores tomorrow. I like being a sloth.

Isn't it amazing how one sin leads to another? I find that this little "sin" test works in almost every kind of discontent. Not everyone goes for the chocolate, of course (although rising obesity rates make a strong case for this one). If you just take a look from a larger perspective, you can pinpoint practically every sin as a major societal trend.

Aside from obesity, there's epidemic consumerism. Think of how many of us are falling prey to gizmos and amusements we don't really need but "have to have." Filling up a hole created by discontent with electronics or clothes doesn't work. Shopping for sport or as a hobby isn't looked upon as a bad thing, but it can definitely be a red flag for discontented behavior.

What about lust? Taboos have broken down to such a degree that it's hard to imagine being seduced by something new. I tend to lust for stuff, feeding that consumer frenzy. But lusty sex is still a place we like to hide, if not just watch, when we are discontented. Isn't that what racy television and Internet sites pick up on? You don't have to act on lust if you can just watch it. Let someone else do the sinning. It's not a sin by association, is it?

Then there's the fascinating push and pull of stocks, bonds, debt, and corporate interests that leave us all to wonder why so much money is in so few hands. Greed is almost a compliment these days. Charity, one of the virtues that counters the sin, is still something found more often in poorer households than in richer ones (people with the lowest incomes tend to give proportionally more to charity). Back to my theory that discontent likes people with money, honey.

Anger is also alive and well and practically acceptable in a large, uncivilized form. The "Make my day" attitude, once celebrated as bold and unique, has broken down to vigilante rigor. There's so much anger floating around, few of us know what to do. Many of us feel underrepresented, underdefended, and ignored by authority. You can read about injustice in the paper every day and feel powerless and voiceless against it; only anger remains. It's fine to be angry now and then, but some people are walking around like grenades ready to detonate. That's explosive societal discontent.

In the end, you can understand sloth. We all have days when we just want to throw in the towel, find a cuddly blanket, and stay in bed. It's so hard to deal with the world; the place is overwhelming. Sloth doesn't sound like sin. It sounds like a reprieve, except that you're not living the life you want, you're escaping the one you hate.

Consider those things that stick in your craw. Recall how easy it is to find fault in the world and how you react to it. Your world, my world, is merely a reflection of all of our energy, our woes, our capabilities. If you're putting out some big discontent, it's going to come back to you. If you're less discontented, the world's going to be a better place. Read on. We can do some nice stuff together.

This Is Not Discontent

I don't want you to think that this book offers you advice for just anything that wrecks your life. It doesn't.

Certain things happen that are just too big for discontent. These events are tragedies, illnesses, losses, or injustices that don't just freeze your life, they transform your life. Untimely death, devastating illness, financial ruin, unjust incarceration—things you cannot anticipate or imagine happening. But they do. These events evoke horror, grief, fear; they take your breath away. They are too big to be just discontent. For these, you will need more than these Instructions to help you.

In some cases, trauma will leave you with residual discontent that these Instructions can handle. In fact, you might find them amusing during your adjustment or healing. However, if you have been leveled by something terrible, find your family, find your faith, find your friends, and hang on. Better days will come.

Preliminary Instructions: Change Tactics

When your world is colored by discontent, you are being coaxed to make some changes. That is the essence of discontent: I didn't feel happy in Wisconsin, so I left. I couldn't find a sense of accomplishment in advertising, so I headed for a new career. It's a lot easier to write those simple sentences than was the actual process I went through to make those changes, and the same will go for you.

All discontent is scratching at you to make some adjustments to your life. You have to make a change to find peace again. This change takes on infinite forms. Change your attitude, change your mind, change your work, your relationships. Deal with your fears. Change is about your whole life and your willingness to bend, stretch, and find new balance for peace inside yourself.

These preliminary Instructions will give you a head start in dealing with your discontent. You can save yourself a great deal of time by knowing how you deal with change and how to improve on your tactics.

The Permanence of Change

Despite the pervasive belief that you can count on certain things in life, everything in your life changes. Your cells are being replaced constantly, your emotions shift at a moment's notice, your prosperity rises and falls, you change your mind from time to time. What doesn't change?

Change is hard for most of us to accept. None of us is truly "Easy come, easy go" when we care deeply about something.

Some change is foreseeable, but that doesn't guarantee that

you'll be able to deal with it smoothly. Other changes are sudden and abrupt. People who have been in accidents will tell you that one moment their life was going along on its usual path, then in one split second it was completely different. My friend Julia got food poisoning and missed her plane to Mexico for a Christmas vacation. She was furious and had to pay a penalty to fly a few days later and was inconvenienced by a difficult connection. That alteration of her plans, that uncomfortable change, put her in the right place at the right time where she met the man who would become her husband. Julia will be the first to tell you that hardship can be your best friend.

Some change is self-created, where you consciously put yourself in a position to transform your life. Some people move to new jobs or homes or even cities to "make a change." Of course, the *real* issues tag along in a suitcase. If the real need for change is in dealing with relationships, you'll be dealing with relationships in your new job, home, or city. If you have money issues, they'll still be there. Your discontent just has a new address.

Change is the opportunity to evolve. And it can be painful. Whether you embrace it too quickly, with the gusto of an old-fashioned beer commercial, or too slowly, drawing the steps out so painfully that your life shifts into slow motion, you still have to pace transitions and straddle disequilibrium to get settled into the other side of that change.

Many Magnitudes of Change

It doesn't really matter what the change is about. Letting go of your vintage teapot collection is painful, but how does it stack up to other kinds of change, such as losing your nose to frostbite or finding your business partner cheated you? Change can take any form and appear in your life in small, efficient doses or huge, rollicking earthquakes. It's always there. Don't be fooled into thinking that you're done with it.

When bad change comes upon you, including discontent, you will want to deny it until you have to face it, curse it until you have forgiven it. Change is a door that opens into a new part of you. You are more resourceful, more intelligent, deeper than you know. Change brings your strength out by challenging you.

THE FUNDAMENTAL RE-BELIEF OF CHANGE

Change is an agent of spirit, not bad luck or God-sent punishment.
෴It might be painful but it's temporary and usually leaves you in a different if not better place than you were before. The great thing about being in the middle of a painful period is knowing that things are always changing—and that means you'll be out of that pain one day.

Let's take a broken heart. If you've ever had a broken heart, you will know that it can be physically painful. Of course, you're emotionally upset, but you also have an ache in your heart. You wonder if you'll ever feel better. When you do meet the right one, you realize that the broken heart has been totally healed and you can say, "Thank goodness I didn't stay with that one because then I would never have met the right one."

Sometimes a single change can stir deeper issues and bring about great change. When I was in my twenties, one of my serious broken hearts left me in a puddle. I watched so many of my friends marry while I did time in bridesmaid's dresses. It hurt to feel so single almost as much as it did to have a broken heart.

Because of that broken heart, I went to see my first astrologer. I was slightly skeptical at the time but I was willing to try anything to feel better. I was told all sorts of things about myself—most of them curiously true. I was gratified to learn that I had talents beyond my current job, and that I would have another career one day. I learned a lot and I felt an enormous sense of relief because a total stranger told me so many things that were accurate already, then asserted that I was going to be married and have a child one day. I would get what I wanted, but not right away.

Because I was so impressed by that astrological reading, I bought a book on astrology and taught myself how to read my chart. One of my motives was to find another way to interpret my love life so that I would be "happily ever after" sooner. My discontent propelled me into studying astrology and becoming adept at interpreting charts beyond my own. It literally changed the way I perceived others and eventually contributed to my career change. My discontent proved to be a positive force.

Unhappiness also opened me up to meditation, the only place I could find peace. I wanted to change my life. I wanted to change my destiny. I studied and experimented with different ideas. I was completely open to thinking about and experiencing life in a completely different way.

I look back on that chart reading as a turning point. I look at that broken heart as a precursor to the most extraordinary change I've ever encountered. It was a long, bumpy change that picked up speed on different fronts—family, home, friends, and job. But it brought me kicking and screaming into the life I wished for and longed for.

Change is good when it's over. When is it over? I'll get to that.

Five Re-Beliefs for Change Resisters

You need an attitudinal adjustment. If you think change is as painful as passing a kidney stone or giving birth, then you're looking at it the wrong way. If change seems the enemy of all that is good, you never took stock of the changes that came before. They might have seemed bad at the time but they didn't kill you. If you're bitter about a change in your past, you haven't completed the package, you haven't used it to evolve. Remember this:

1. Change is a friend.
2. Not all change is a job for Job.
3. Change has a permanent place in your life.
4. Change is an opportunity to improve your sense of humanity and your sense of humor.
5. Change demands new levels of forgiveness, the path to spiritual ease.

RE-BELIEF #1: CHANGE IS A FRIEND

❧It makes you grow, it opens your heart to *yourself*. If change brings you pain, its purpose is to make you vulnerable. Change resisters don't want to be vulnerable, a great mistake. Being vulnerable isn't weak, it's a way to find your power. Pain breaks down internal defenses. Although pain is personal ("Ouch!"), it's universal. Everyone has his own pain. Stephen Levine, author of *Healing into Life and Death*, says it isn't "your pain," it's "*the* pain." When you're in pain, you're more compassionate to others in pain. It isn't that misery loves company, it's that pain can make you say, "I know what you're going through. I respect what you're going through." Change and the pain it brings are there to show you how strong you are and how powerful your compassion is.

RE-BELIEF #2: NOT ALL CHANGE IS A JOB FOR JOB

❧My early religious education included a full year about Job, the poor man in the Bible whose faith God tested over and over. Some changes, especially when they come in clumps (in "threes," we often think), can feel as if God is testing you. While some changes are more painful than others, you shouldn't consider everything that comes your way as a test. You don't have to indulge in suffering to make change a spiritual process. Change is a way of making you reach inside yourself, of being your own companion, but it doesn't mean you have to cry out in the darkness of the soul. Not every change demands drama of that nature. Most change asks you to deal with something you don't want to face. The key to most change is just saying, "Oh, all right," and finding the room in yourself to accept it without anger, judgment, or conditions.

RE-BELIEF #3: CHANGE HAS A
PERMANENT PLACE IN YOUR LIFE

❧Half the pain of change comes from resisting it. If you accept change as a boarder who sometimes goes to his room for days and sometimes sits at your table demanding attention, you'll feel less afraid of it. When you accept change as a natural part of your life, you won't be so surprised and horrified when it shows up and demands that you come with it.

RE-BELIEF #4: CHANGE IS AN OPPORTUNITY TO IMPROVE YOUR SENSE OF HUMANITY AND YOUR SENSE OF HUMOR

❧Most of the time I delight in telling others about my painful experiences because now I can laugh about them. I can feel compassion for what happened to me and it makes me much more compassionate toward others. Even with the most hellish passages of my life, I can look back and be proud that I made it through them. I learned from change and therefore I can help other people who are going through their own difficult changes. I can hold the faith for others because I learned about doing that all myself. You can, too. You just have to allow the pain to pass and know that the peacefulness, contentment, and sense of empowerment that follow are very agreeable.

RE-BELIEF #5: CHANGE DEMANDS NEW LEVELS OF FORGIVENESS, THE PATH TO SPIRITUAL EASE

❧It starts with acceptance and closes with forgiveness. You can see the process of change as scaling new heights in yourself. Your heart will grow, your tolerance will widen, and your life will flow more easily. The bumps, bruises, and scars in your heart will heal with forgiveness, and you are both deeper and lighter as a result.

Changing Styles

In astrology, three different categories describe how a person deals with change. These modes are defined by the sign you are born under. The cardinal signs introduce a new season, with Aries being the first sign of spring, Cancer for summer, Libra for autumn, and Capricorn for winter. The fixed signs know only one season and don't have to adjust to change, such as Taurus (spring), Leo (summer), Scorpio (autumn), and Aquarius (winter). The mutable signs are the last sign of a season. They are open to change as their season comes to an end, as Gemini ends spring, Virgo ends summer, Sagittarius ends autumn, and Pisces ends winter.

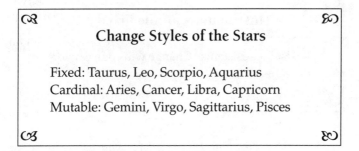

Change Styles of the Stars

Fixed: Taurus, Leo, Scorpio, Aquarius
Cardinal: Aries, Cancer, Libra, Capricorn
Mutable: Gemini, Virgo, Sagittarius, Pisces

Fixed: The Great Resistance

Those of you who fall under the "fixed" mode are stubborn. You're probably chuckling because I'm right. You don't deal with change for a long, long time. People might look at you and wonder why you don't just do it (fill in the blank with whatever change you're resisting). I have many friends who are fixed and I find them exasperating. I listened to one very fixed girlfriend complain about her husband and their lack of affection, understanding, communication, passion, and mutual support for over *seven* years before she did anything about it. They had no children, and every year that passed, she lost more time in finding the right relationship. The first attempt, after seven years, to improve her life was marriage counseling. She attended that alone for a year for even more proof that her marriage wasn't working. It thus took her eight years to leave him, another two to find a better relationship.

That's the story of a very fixed person. Some of these people are ostriches who put their heads in the sand to stay blind to the change ahead. Some are just frozen in the face of change, and some dare change to take them by force.

If you're fixed, you'll enjoy these Instructions. Think about them for a long time, and use them whenever the mood moves you. If you don't use them at all, your change is going to be prolonged and painful, and your discontent will settle in for a nice long visit.

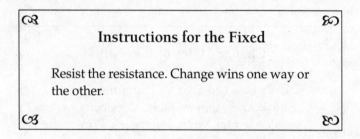

Instructions for the Fixed

Resist the resistance. Change wins one way or the other.

Cardinal: I'll Do It My Way

Cardinal approaches are like the flight of an arrow: with great force and purpose, the arrow takes off straight in one direction. When change approaches, you form your action plan and execute it without second-guessing. Usually, you employ accuracy before speed so that your plan is carried out without a problem. But if you're off by a single degree, your arrow will miss its target and you will have exerted all your energy in vain. This is not only frustrating, but can lead to a sense of powerlessness and failure. Cardinal energy is aimed at success, and when it meets with failure, a great deal of reevaluation is required.

Cardinal approaches to change are effective when you have the right target in sight. But you have to be clear about your goal, and discontent can easily cloud your vision. It can cause you to take aim at a place in your life that doesn't really need fixing.

I have a close friend who is a high-level executive at an advertising firm. She is one of the best strategic thinkers and problem-solvers in her industry—that's the great cardinal energy going right for the bull's-eye. Unfortunately, the advertising industry has recently been going through a series of contractions and difficulties that keep squeezing out people—even smart ones like my friend.

As her job got tougher, smaller, and harder to negotiate, she kept slinging those arrows to tackle the problems—with people, with production, with impossible deadlines—even as they became insurmountable. Instead of looking outside her world and noticing the greater changes and opportunities, she focused more energy on what was on her desk. It didn't work. Her unhappiness with her work was at an all-time high. Her job ended. Being cardinal, she picked herself up, worked on understanding the events of the past that had caused her to lose her job, and began charting a new future using that same solve-it-and-get-it-done energy.

Cardinal approaches to change are extremely effective when you understand the real message behind the discontent. Don't beat yourself up if your arrow hits the wrong target. Few of us possess the kind of clarity and dispassion it takes to immediately identify and dig up the real roots of discontent in our daily lives.

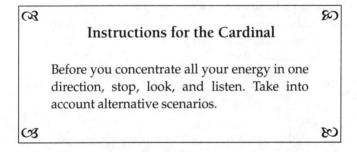

Instructions for the Cardinal

Before you concentrate all your energy in one direction, stop, look, and listen. Take into account alternative scenarios.

Mutable: Which Way Do I Go? I'll Try Them All

Those of you who are mutable in your approach to change are ready to hopscotch diagonally across any kind of path. The hard part is standing still and understanding exactly where you should go. Mutability is the attention deficit disorder of discontent.

Those of us who are more mutable like variety. You'll find that, for instance, if you want to improve your self-esteem, you might try a diet, a tennis camp, joining Toastmasters, or volunteering at your local Salvation Army. Mutable approaches, however, often don't last long enough to work. Or if you do get results, you won't necessarily know why. That means you'll get another opportunity to learn (that's another change, another discontent).

I am the poster child for the mutable approach. Once discontent hits me, I'll wriggle in any direction I can to find a way out. I'll buy books, take a class, search on-line, talk to friends, get second opinions. Recently I tried to lose weight (improve self-esteem). I cooked new, lower-fat recipes, talked with friends about the diets that had worked for them, surfed dieting and weight-loss Web sites—you name it, I did it all, except lose weight. I know how to do that—eat less and exercise more—but I took my time before I focused. Mutability is disruptive when you deal with discontent because it distracts you from the basic issue. Once I get close to something that works, I get bored (or scared) and move on to something else. Mutability almost compels you to stay in discontent because it gives you something to do. Mutability likes to be busy and, in some ways, doesn't trust times of contentment because they might be boring. This is a tough lesson for mutable people.

Mutability is moving too much, too fast, to let the discontent tell you what needs your attention.

Instructions for the Mutable

Wait it out. Before you try something new, give yourself another week. The urge to move on will pass.

Finding Yourself

Some of you immediately felt at home in one of these categories. But if you feel your astrological sign doesn't match your way of dealing with change, don't worry. The next time you have the opportunity to learn through discontent and the change it demands, you'll have a better idea of just what kind of approach you like to use.

As you use these Instructions, keep in mind that you will integrate them into your life differently from other people. Digest this information and dissolve your discontent in the way that works best for you. There is no time limit on using these Instructions, nor is there a statute of limitations on your discontent.

What's It All About?
Karma, Power, and Fear

It is important to understand the relationship of karma, power, and fear because they will answer a lot of your questions as you go through these Instructions. Karma, power, and fear are interrelated energies that captivate, control, challenge, and sometimes destroy things in your life (for a reason) and demand that you change. Relationships, jobs, the way you feel about yourself—your significant experiences in life are invariably composed of these three components fiddling around to test, strengthen, and finalize exactly how you will evolve.

Karma, power, and fear are closely aligned, so don't feel frustrated if you fail to see clear boundaries among them. They work together to make you face changes that are necessary for your happiness. They weave through your life to bring you discontent so that you can eventually be happier.

Karma

Some of you might be familiar with the concept of karma and the role it plays in relationships and other aspects of life.

Karma is essentially the idea that what you are and what happens to you (and whom you meet and the family you are born with) are the result of all other actions and choices, deeds and opportunities, from your previous lives. It's a little like the law of conservation of energy, where every action has an equal and opposite reaction—except that your actions in this life might have reactions in the next. Some people consider the law of karma more like the Golden Rule: Do unto others as you would have them do unto you. What you put out, you get back.

Even in this life, you are acting out karma and creating it. I imagine that perfection, i.e., no karma or karmic debt, is beyond us mere mortals. Karma is the road to spiritual evolution. We are all toiling away on that road, bumping into each other with our bad karma or hitching a lift with the good stuff.

A job can be karmic; I can attest to that. In my unhappy corporate career, I used to consult card readers and channelers and all sorts of "seers" who would, I hoped, shed light on a career that would be more fulfilling. I was constantly told that my karma was to work with ancient things or beliefs and to be a bridge between the modern world and ancient wisdom. I didn't understand what these predictions were until I found myself doing astrological chart readings and writing books about ancient beliefs, intuition, and psychic power. I am a bridge—walk over me and see into your own karma.

Your karma is inescapable. It will take you on necessary life adventures to bring you closer to your purpose and a life of fulfillment. It will give you chances to work out issues or problems you have—with people, with money, even with pets. Your karma creates many opportunities to grow into a fully actualized individual.

Power

Power is about your free will and the opportunity to exercise it. Power can be used to influence others, but that's not true power. You are born with the innate power to choose what you want in life. While at first your parents shape your power with their choices for you, eventually you don't need them to do that. When you reach adulthood, you are vested with your own power and it's time to understand what that really means, and to use it wisely.

It's not that simple, though. Few of us reach the age of eighteen or twenty-one and feel perfectly free to pursue our dreams, even though we are considered mature enough to do so.

Power is hard to get used to. Even as an adult you might look to your parents, friends, or partners for approval. While you do have power, life demands that you share it, entrust it to others (as in electing officials to make choices for you), and use it to give someone else a chance. Power is negotiable in almost all parts of life.

Learning how to use your power wisely is a lifelong challenge. Most of us spend a great deal of our adulthood trying to feel our power, exercise it, and maintain its integrity. Karma brings you ample opportunities to try it out.

Fear

You can't escape that fear is a part of life. Fear is embedded in human nature; its most basic function is to keep us out of harm's way—to preserve life. But fear works its way into less obvious places, such as relationships (fear of getting hurt), work (fear of being fired or undervalued), travel (fear of accidents), and so on. You can be afraid of just about anything.

Fear works well to cap your power and keep you from making choices that will better your life. You can let fear keep you stuck in a less fulfilling career simply because you're afraid to exercise your power and try something else. Fear can keep you in bad relationships, too. There isn't a corner of your life that fear can't penetrate and press upon you to stay put—for safety's sake. In these cases, fear is the excuse you use to let go of your power. And you'll have fear to thank for keeping you frozen in discontent.

Whereas power needs to be integrated into your being, fear is something you must learn to disperse. Instead of perceiving a solid wall of terror, you can learn to loosen fear's energy and pass through it as if it were a thin curtain of fog.

Fear is fine to keep you alert. It's better than caffeine. But if you let your life be overtaken by fear, your power will dim, your karmic path will stagnate, and you'll lose the many opportunities to open up to happiness. No fear, except a realistic fear of danger, can be worth that much sacrifice.

*   *   *

Instructions for Your Discontent

The Instructions that follow are to help you on your karmic journey, to encourage you to feel your power and exercise it wisely, and to dismantle walls of fear that impede your passage to the ultimate goal: a happy life.

Part I

$

Prosperity

The most frequent and accessible form of discontent concerns prosperity. We live in a materially focused society and it is acceptable (within reason) to discuss money, achievement, property, and wealth. We are continually bombarded with information and advertising to "buy this" or "sell that," "make more money" or "invest here." We're more comfortable discussing prices and costs than relationships and love problems. Money and prosperity is an acceptable form of discontent and certainly one that visits us all from time to time.

No one, no matter how wealthy, is immune to prosperity discontent. Whether or not you are prosperous has little to do with your net worth.

The first stop and arguably the most commonly held discontent is about money, property, and dreams of more.

Money and Property

How often do you think, "If I only had more money, everything would be easier"? You dream of winning Powerball or the lottery. You think that being able to afford everything you want would make your life better. You could pay off your house and feel more secure. You could pay for your child's college education, better health care for your family, and take more exotic vacations. Sure, money will accomplish these things, but it won't dissolve your discontent and it won't make your prosperity problems disappear. Having money doesn't mean you're content with prosperity.

Even if you become a billionaire and set up foundations to save the world, you won't be immune to prosperity discontent. If it's an issue now, it will be an issue then. The wealthy are probably even more acutely exposed to discontent because of all that money. The world is watching, waiting for them to mess up. Even if they do manage to avoid the public eye, they can't escape the creeping grip of discontent.

To dissolve discontent about money, property, and possessions, you must dismantle some assumptions you've made about prosperity. You'll need a Re-Belief.

The Ancient Story of Security

Let's go back to earliest civilization as we know it, to a time when our ancestors lived as hunter/gatherers. They got hungry and went after food and kept warm with the skins of animals they'd hunted. It was a simple life of survival, without minor irritations such as answering e-mail and remembering PIN numbers, or major setbacks such as losing a job or forfeiting a mortgage. They had to find food, shelter, and stay out of the way of predators. That's it. Eventually, those hunters began to settle down to farm the land. They learned to grow food, even trade what they produced with others. Prosperity came in the form of good crops and friendly trades. Was there always enough to go around? Probably not, but they learned to survive.

These societies eventually got more complicated. Someone got to be the leader, a chieftain or king or queen. There was a spiritual leader, and perhaps some families had more and some had less. Still, they functioned. People ate, lived, and had children.

Survival issues were now less pressing and people had the luxury of being more concerned with their security and comfort. Instead of just getting fed, keeping warm, and making babies, our ancestors started getting pretty tetchy about borders, about who owned which fertile valley. The leaders built castles and fortresses to keep marauders from taking their stuff. If one tribe or society had a bad harvest, they went looking for food elsewhere.

That's when the trouble started. Those people who still had food and shelter didn't want to share it, out of fear that there wouldn't be enough to go around. And the other people, the ones who had a bad harvest . . . well, let's just say that people get pretty desperate when they're hungry and they'll do almost anything to get food. Instead of sitting down and thinking with clear heads that more hands in the fields might produce more food and how a society created out of two tribes would benefit, the hungry got warriorlike and the mentality of "I want what you have but we both can't have it" was born.

This is my own admittedly oversimplified version of world history and economics. Yet we still live with this same mentality when we fear that someone will take away our stuff or there's not enough to go around. Those two mind-sets will keep you feeling discontent.

In those ancient times, people were kept safe by kings or chieftains who provided security for a price: "Work my land for me, give me the profits, and in turn my soldiers will protect you." There was no guarantee, really, that this leader would be completely effective, but the illusion of safety, of belonging, of having a place in society, was enough to keep most of our ancestors pretty . . . content? Perhaps not that, but certainly alive and less worried.

Until a few years ago, this mentality prevailed. Work for a corporation. Hand over the fruits of your labor to the guys who own the company. Get "safety" in the form of a paycheck, insurance, a retirement plan. Everyone was happy. Today, unfortunately, most of the corporations don't make such promises. They certainly can't protect you. There are layoffs without safety nets. And our fears grow even more acute.

Who will protect us?

Who will feed us?

Who will make sure the marauders—the bankers—don't steal our home?

The root of your prosperity discontent is in your belief that a safe place exists.

PROSPERITY RE-BELIEF #1

There is no safe place, and no amount of money or property can buy it.

❧ Not a single soul or place on this earth guarantees you a life protected from your fears. I tell you this because once you stop looking for safety, you can start releasing your discontent. You'll stop looking for the Holy Grail of protection and begin living in the flow of your own abundance. You do have it, you know.

PROSPERITY RE-BELIEF #2

There is enough to go around.

❧ Given the surpluses in America and other countries, there is plenty of food in the world. There are enough resources. They're just not distributed evenly.

We are constantly told that the entire world could be fed if we could only distribute the food to those who need it. The news shows us gut-wrenching famine in Ethiopia, in Sudan, in Kenya, in Afghanistan. Those people don't have to starve; there's enough food on the planet. But we don't send it to them because, aside from the issue of who is going to pay for it, there's a little part of us that says, "If they get strong enough, they'll come and take our stuff." Food can be used as a powerful pawn in international relations, but there is no truth to scarcity. Erase it from your consciousness.

If you readjust your prosperity consciousness so you don't immediately leap to "there's not enough to go around," you'll make a bigger impact on everyone than just sending $20 to a relief organization (although you should do that, too). If you stop thinking "Someone's going to take my stuff," you might inspire others to stop, too. Not only will you set a good example, but you'll also contribute to a more generous, healing consciousness. If you avoid the "not enough" idea, you'll be able to take more risks in your life and follow your contented heart to your own prosperity.

When I was in my early twenties, I had the startling pleasure and discomfort of watching my sixty-four-year-old cousin, Svetlana, come to visit the United States from Moscow during perestroika (when the Cold War was only just thawing). This woman had very little "stuff" in her life and had known perilously dark periods of famine and fear, having lived through Stalin's Russia. I took her to a little grocery store in New York. It was not a supermarket, price club, or wholesaler, just a corner deli that sold everything you'd need at the last minute (and for a premium price). As she walked down the aisles with me, she got sick to her stomach and had to leave. She'd never seen such abundance or variety. In Moscow, the stores were virtually empty, and if they did have anything at all, it was one item and nothing else. No choice. No flavors. No food.

I reevaluated my perception of abundance and will always remember her shock at seeing what we take for granted every day.

There *Is* Enough to Go Around

In the interest of full disclosure, note that I've been participating in this "enough to go around" belief for more than thirteen years. I'm the first to admit that I'm not rich and that I've had some pretty scary scrapes with menacingly low bank balances. And I'm not immune to the fears of not having "enough" and the occasional burning desire to be stinking, filthy rich. But it has all worked out. Most of the time, I know I have enough: my health, my family, a home, time to myself and to do the work I love, a baby-sitter when we need it. I try not to let my life or peace of mind get immersed in prosperity discontent, but it's definitely a work in progress. Even if *you* believe there is enough to go around, many people don't, and their fear can permeate your life. To live in prosperity ease, you have to keep going back to the belief of abundance, not scarcity.

What's Enough?

At one stage of my life, when I had very little money, a woman I worked with married a wealthy man. She was low-key about her situation and his abundance. I once asked why she still worked and she admitted that she didn't feel comfortable unless she had at least $100,000 in her bank account (of her own money), and even that wasn't enough to make her feel completely secure. That amount was a king's ransom to my poor ears—it still is. I would have felt comfortable with $1,000 in the bank.

It's a natural reaction to hold on tight to what you have, especially if you think "There's not enough to go around." A man I know displays this by not turning on any lights in his house during the day for fear people will see what he has in his house and want to steal it. When I visit, I *beg* him to turn on the lights because it's too depressing sitting in the dark. He'll close his curtains and seal the place before turning on a light.

I tease him mercilessly about this. There is little crime in his town and burglaries are practically unheard of, so who will go through the trouble of studying his house, cataloging what there is to steal, and making the effort (and risking the consequences) to steal it? Furthermore, if someone did break into his house and steal his property, would he survive? Sure. Even the queen won't keel over if someone helps himself to the crown jewels of England. She might be angry or sad, but she won't die from it.

The only material possessions you have to worry about are

your physical body and your roof. If your body is out of whack, you have reason to be discontented. If your home is threatened, you must confront issues of survival and safety. These are basic needs that must be met, and your bad mood is worthy of the situation.

If you're just worried about your possessions, as in how you're going to pay for the unnecessary but beautiful imported kitchen tiles, you're suffering from discontent. Some people like to test their tolerance level for debt and risk by living with a large overhead and shifting funds to cover payments every month. If you like to gamble that way, be my guest. But it's not my idea of fun.

Wealth is certainly a relative term. My grandmother considered sugar and cream like gold long after rationing for World War II had stopped. She felt a great sense of abundance simply having them in her home. My father felt wealthy because he paid off his mortgage and owned his house outright. He was a "landowner" and had earned the title. On the other side, I have friends who only fly first class and think real wealth is owning a private jet. Wealth is relative to your current situation. How much is enough?

Your "enough" is found in the trust you have toward prosperity whether it's high or low. You always know there is—and there will be—enough.

Karma, Power, and Fear: A Prosperity Checkup

In those cases where you really do have to worry about money, as in making your mortgage payments or sustaining unforeseen expenses through no fault of your own, you don't have immediate concerns about karma/power/fear implications. You do have to get going to deal with practical solutions and endure the discontent of the problems, but you don't have to reprogram your beliefs or revisit issues about prosperity—unless you keep coming up on the same problems over and over. That's when you look at karma, power, and fear.

If you don't have prosperity problems but still have prosperity discontent, you will have to check up on your connections. Karma, power, and fear are very much alive and well and contributing to your discontent.

ROOTS OF PROSPERITY-RELATED DISCONTENT

Hidden Belief	Who's Responsible
I'll worry about money my whole life.	Karma/fear
I'll never have what I really want.	Power
I'd rather not take any risks and be safe, not sorry.	Fear

Karma

Because karma is hard to pin down precisely, chronic paranoia about money may indicate you did not have enough in a prior life, or conversely, you squandered wealth then and are only now dealing with the consequences. It's pointless to argue how much karma affects your prosperity issues, but it's useful to consider it as a factor. It takes the pressure off diagnosing why you are the way you are (was it your Depression-era grandmother? That your father squandered the family fortune? That you didn't buy AOL stock when you had the chance?) and allows you to concentrate on fixing it. And you *can* fix it.

Karma is not an excuse to stay troubled. Release the chains of karma by participating more actively in your life. Your karmic issues dissipate once you face them, and to face them you must access and use your power.

It's more likely that your relationship to power and fear is at the crux of your prosperity discontent. We live in a culture that puts a lot of emphasis on money as power. If you don't have a lot of money, you might think that you don't have power, which is a false belief. Fear is different. Fear is necessary in our lives to the extent that it cautions us from real danger, as in basic survival. Fear about money, though, isn't likely to be a real survival issue. Fear and worry about money are not about staying alive, but a sign of a deeper discontent.

The Power of Money

Money is not power, it is buying power. Remember, personal power is your ability to influence the world around you. You can have little money or wealth and still have great personal power, such as Mother Teresa had in her lifetime. Money and the things it can buy can be tools to help you use your personal power, but they are not the only tools available to you. If you think that your power is tied up with the amount of money you have, you will become a slave to your bank account, and while you're concentrating on acquiring more money, you will miss a whole lot of life experiences and pleasures. That is not at all powerful. If you are working out karma and need to exercise your power more consciously, you're going to have to start trusting yourself and the universe to provide for you. While your bank account reflects what you've earned, your contentment is a true sign of your prosperity.

PROSPERITY RE-BELIEF #3

Abundance comes from the ability to live the life you want.
❧Get clear: power is your ability to make choices; then exercise those choices. Pursue your dreams. Listen to your heart. Live a life that you help to create. You will feel blessed with abundance when you are able to live out your dreams. That's true wealth. You won't notice or care whether your neighbor bought a new Lexus if you finally allow yourself to learn oil painting or bricklaying or whatever you really, really want to do.

Fear

We can harbor fears about money in countless ways. You can be afraid of losing it, not having enough of it, never being able to get enough of it, and any combination thereof. You can even have an endless amount of money, more than you could spend in a lifetime, and be afraid of its implications—how to use it responsibly, who your real friends are, who might want to "use" you. Fears are irrational and infinite. This is only the beginning.

To conquer any fear, you must revisit your values and choose what is truly important to you and what is not.

Fear is tricky. It keeps you from spending, making, and enjoying money. In some ways, fear is a necessary evil—it keeps you from taking risks you can't afford. But fear should be limited in your decision-making, not the last and final stop. When fear is the reason you don't do something, even something as trivial as shopping in a mall or getting on a bus, you're in trouble. Your life will get small and your choices will dry up if you let fear take over.

BASIC PROSPERITY INSTRUCTION

Keep your hand open so that things can fall into it.

❧ Tightfisted attitudes about money only breed more emotional and psychological tightness, which makes less room for you to experience abundance. Put the squeeze on what you want and watch it crumble in your hand. You've probably experienced the searing disappointment of not getting something you really wanted. That's from putting too much energy around it, too much single-minded "gotta have it" and not allowing for other possibilities. When your hand is open, when your energy is dancing on desire but not intent on *must have it*, you may get it—or you might get something even better.

Worry Not

You actually have a choice in how much you worry. You might be worried about money simply because that's what your parents did. You might be worried about taking risks because you have no prior experience with it. Worry is a waste of your time and emotional energy; it is unproductive and will not prevent an event from happening but it will erode your potential for happiness. Keep worrying and you'll never have what you want.

Practically Speaking

If you really are concerned about your prosperity, educate yourself. The more you know about managing money and investments, risks and returns, the less you'll worry. You need to take back your power and work on getting what you want instead of sitting back and taking the lumps. You have as much freedom to choose what you do with yourself and your prosperity as anyone else.

Insecurity and Securities

The stock market was once explained to me with astonishing clarity by my metaphysics teacher, Julie Winter. We were studying prosperity at the time, and a few weeks into the class there was a market correction (or crash, as some call it). She explained that the stock market is just a symbol of value, a product of what we all believe. If we think a company will grow and make money, the stock price will rise because everyone wants a piece of it. Does this mean the company will make more money? No. Does this mean we'll always believe that this company is good? No. Will this guarantee you a return? No. The stock market is a product of group belief. When you buy stock, you are investing not in the company itself, but in the belief about the future of that company.

As an astrologer with a large business clientele, I see a lot of fear and concern about money and the stock market. I see joy and excitement when the market is good, and fear and melancholy as it subsides. Even though economists continually support the theory that we have business cycles and that growth is going to be countered by recession, we are still surprised by the downside. During an economic slide, some of my clients look like forlorn children at the end of Christmas—they can't believe it's over.

The lesson I love to learn and teach (again and again) is to trust the flow of prosperity. It comes and goes. Life is a cycle. Nature is a cycle. So why does everyone get so caught up in the ups and downs of prosperity when it's pretty much proven that ups and downs are part of the deal? You can't keep expanding; contractions are natural. You'll probably have a prosperous life with a few downturns, as we all have. Losing a job (one kind of downturn) is not a permanent low. Getting into debt doesn't mean you'll make bad financial decisions forever. Not making a lot of money has nothing to do with being fulfilled or happy in your life. Your money and prosperity ups and downs are natural. It's how you approach them that makes or breaks your discontent.

That is the little trick to prosperity. Live in the flow of what you have, allow more to come, allow some to go, and enjoy what you have right now instead of wishing for what you could have had or what you might be getting.

Tithing

The Bible says you should give part of what you make to those less fortunate. The accepted interpretation is about 10 percent of your income. You can interpret this literally and give 10 percent of what you have to your church, or you can broadly interpret the concept of giving back. Consider how and what you want to give. Is it money? Time spent doing volunteer work? Time spent in prayer or meditation? Those are all giving situations where you put aside your own life for a moment and focus your energy toward others.

I feel sad for people who don't have room for prayer or meditation in their life. They miss a personal, powerful, and direct connection to an amazing universal energy, but more important, they don't know the meaning of grace. Prayer isn't only to be used when dealing with frightening circumstances. It's a way of watering your spiritual garden, a form of soul health.

I feel that prayer or meditation is a form of tithing because the more people who consciously connect to this greater power, the more likely we will all benefit from it. Prayer can bring on healing in its many forms. It can affect greater things than your personal life or someone's health (although these are perfectly lovely effects of prayer). When a lot of us join together to put out our energy—call it love or awe or heart connection—we form a powerful current. Prayer and meditation are antidotes for greed and coveting. Meditation can help you feel more complete, and when you feel complete, you don't lust for more.

When I talk about prayer as a tithe or charitable act, I'm not talking about prayer for getting your own way. The kind of tithe prayer I'm suggesting is not self-centered, as in "Please, God, can I have that promotion?" A tithe prayer is sent without a return address. For example: "I ask the universe to send love and healing to all those souls who need it, and to open the hearts of all beings to love and peace."

Giving freely to others is a way to demonstrate to yourself and to the universe that you participate in the flow of prosperity and that you know what comes and goes is part of the great cycle. Giving freely often brings in more. Try it. Tithe in some form and see how it comes back to you. It's one of those great kickbacks you get in life.

A little note for parents: if you or your child shows signs of discontent, try volunteering together. You'll set a great example and share a nice experience. My teenage baby-sitter and her mother are talking about working on a house for Habitat for Humanity as part of their summer vacation. It's a terrific way to pitch in and help others while doing something fun and keeping tabs on what's going on in your kid's head.

Property

I'm a chronic real estate coveter. I read real estate circulars listing residences all over Manhattan. My husband and I call it the Envy Catalog. I scour the real estate newspaper ads every weekend, watching the prices go up or down. I hear about other people buying a home, adding on to their home, or just redecorating, and my discontent zooms to the surface.

If you've been taking in what I've said so far, you're going to tell me to get on it, face my discontent, and take action: buy a place or move to something else. There are plenty of neighborhoods we can afford. Our accountant is always telling us to move to the suburbs.

Money and Property

You're right. He's right. But we won't because my husband's commute would be terrible. I accept my real estate discontent because I refuse a move that would value space and money over the time we spend together. I will not elect to live in a home that isn't exactly what I desire, so I am the master of my discontent.

I try to laugh about it. We call our small apartment the Mouse House. Every inch of space has been studied for its potential usefulness, and we have grown accustomed to moving furniture to open closets. I have artwork I love under our bed because our wall space has given way to bookshelves. It makes me appreciate how much stuff I have and makes me reluctant to buy anything we don't need.

Now here's what we get for staying put. Our rent is reasonable, which doesn't put pressure on me to earn a steady salary—a comfort to any author. Because we live in the city, we don't own a car, so we don't use much energy or have a car payment. And the best part of our small home is that we are always around each other. Of course this can also get on our nerves, but intimacy and sharing are easier and more natural because we tend to cluster together most mornings and evenings. Sure we want to have more space and surely one day we will, but for now, we're here.

There's nothing wrong with wanting a home of your own, or even a larger home, but a big house on the fanciest street won't dissolve your discontent. Your home is what you make of it. Your joy, life force, and energy can infuse your home with contentment. You can live in Buckingham Palace and still be grumpy. I can live in tiny quarters with a husband, our child, and a fat cat and find it cozy and lovely.

The long and short of real estate discontent is to make the most of the home you've got. Dream, if you must, of a better or bigger house, but don't ignore the place you call home now. It's where your life is.

More Is Not Enough: What You Own

We live in amazing times. You can set your digital, waterproof watch to nanoseconds, and by the time you do, the next level of technology, convenience, and provisions will unfold. My grand-mother was born before telephones and radios were common and just before the first car. She died in the age of personal computers. I was born when record albums were played, which turned into eight-track players, which transformed into cassettes, and then CDs. This was before cable television, satellites, and the all-important beeper/pager/cell-phone explosion. I learned chemistry using a slide rule; now pocket calculators are in every child's backpack. Personal computers didn't exist in my youth; now I can't live without e-mail.

This gives us a little perspective on how fast "stuff" changes and how quickly we buy into the next new thing. And I don't need to tell you that we don't really need any of it. By that I mean that we don't need a computer or a DVD player to live a healthy, happy life.

What we consider "staples" in our lives—a cell phone and a sound system, for example—aren't really crucial at all. Sure, they're nice, but will adding to or upgrading your appliances and equipment make you feel less discontent?

Stuff for Discontent

Filling your life with stuff doesn't make you feel rich or prosper-ous. Being constantly acquisitive actually increases discontent and decreases your bank balance. Chronic shopping is as addictive and potentially damaging as drug addiction.

If you find that you are stuffing your life with material things, you're trying to treat discontent with shopping therapy. This is an expensive, ineffective method of dealing with life's bigger issues. Having stuff won't make your love life better. Having stuff won't keep you healthy or happy. Having stuff won't give you more time to do what you love or relieve your anger or frustration.

How about you? Are you a chronic shopper? What's your weakness? Is it a stress reducer or a life filler?

When I find myself enjoying a good three hours perusing the well-stocked, appetizing aisles of my favorite discount store, I know I'm self-medicating my discontent. My husband does the same thing in used-book stores. We might spend a little money, but it's never more than we can afford, which is the key. We know when to quit.

If you shop for more than you can afford, you have serious discontent. If you shop for sport and don't overpurchase, you're within the healthy zone. I don't expect that you'll quit shopping and I know I won't. But I do suggest that you become conscious of your motives, your emotional state, and your bank balance when you shop, so that your discontent doesn't get the better of you. Shopping for sport shouldn't be your only outside activity.

INSTRUCTIONS FOR THE STUFF OF DISCONTENT

❧ If you find that you want to cut down on the needless possessions that weave their way into your life, think about diverting that energy into something that you can produce and expand. Grow something. I don't care if it's a Chia Pet. Watch a plant grow from a seed, a tree from a sapling, a bush from a cutting. I have no garden, but every spring I perform a growing ritual on the day of the spring equinox. I just plant a seed for a window-box plant and enjoy watching it grow from shoots to flowers.

The point of gardening is to reconnect your desire for "stuff" with something that is basic and satisfying, not to mention good for the planet. You can still buy a huge TV and keep our economy strong. You'll just do it in a more conscious, less hungry way.

Unstuffing

When you're ready to simplify or de-stuff your life, consider giving away what you no longer want or need. Sure, you can sell it, but how easy it is to tithe instead. Plenty of people don't have much stuff and would be grateful for yours. Release your excess to those who need it and live lighter, less burdened, and less complicated. You'll also be less discontent.

Employment

IT wouldn't be fair to address prosperity discontent without addressing unemployment. Once a state of disgrace, unemployment has become an all-too-familiar part of life. At any point in your career, you could find yourself laid off, fired, or downsized. Or you could quit a job before finding another one. Unemployment isn't taboo anymore, it's a reality as businesses and services adjust to economic change.

Although unemployment is an acceptable state of transition, you can still be in for some major discontent. If you're unemployed longer than you'd anticipated, for instance, or if you feel that you were unfairly treated, you will experience varying degrees of discontent, and that can hinder reemployment. We want to nip that in the bud.

My personal experience with unemployment was voluntary. When pushed to an intolerable degree of stress and discontent, I quit my job to pursue a writing career for which I had no promise of income. Although leaving my job was my idea, it helped my former employers cut costs. They agreed to consider me "laid off" and I collected unemployment.

My unemployment experience was gentler than the stories I've heard about sudden firings, security escorts, and less than an hour's notice before finding yourself on the street. Abrupt or smooth, unemployment is a strange state of affairs.

If you've been fired or if your layoff came as a surprise, you're going to go through a period similar to mourning a loss. Disbelief comes first. How could this happen? Once the shock is absorbed, there is grief fueled by the rejection, the implied "We don't want you here" from your former company. Eventually you get angry— which can be healthy. The circumstances merit your anger to an extent. Unless you were fired for "cause," doing something wrong on the job, you can be angry at the injustice of the situation. All of these reactions to job loss can be eased by counseling—friends or therapists—but experiencing these emotions is crucial to moving on with your life and your career.

It can take a while to come to terms with being jobless. You no longer hold a position that identifies you as an employee, as someone with a connection to an organization. This can be troubling if your self-esteem is entrenched in your work. You may question your identity as well as your worth, which can lead to more problems. Shift your focus from loss to opportunity and you won't succumb to those dark self-doubts.

UNEMPLOYMENT RE-BELIEF

Unemployment is your chance to reinvent and improve your relationship to work and prosperity.

❧ Unemployment in its purest sense is a highly creative state. All of a sudden a major part of your identity is gone, and the thing that occupied most of your time has evaporated. You're left with a whole lot of room on your calendar and a thoughtful pause when someone asks, "What do you do?" I spent six months answering that question with "I used to be an advertising executive," because saying "I'm an unpublished writer" was too scary. Not knowing how to answer that question is like being asked, "What do you want to be when you grow up?" You have a chance to pursue your dreams.

Being unemployed allowed me the time to conceive of and sell an idea for a book, and to transition into my new title, "author." I knew I wanted to write. You might not know what you want to do with all that time, though. It can feel awkward and foreign to be unscheduled and undercommitted.

And then there's the money thing.

I was lucky that I had no financial obligations that loomed over me right away. I did, however, become afraid because it took much longer to make a publishing deal than I had anticipated. If you're jobless and things seem to be taking time to sort out, you might get to know a little prosperity discontent. That's what I'm here for.

Prosperity Assessments

If you get laid off or if you're between jobs, you must adjust your prosperity to keep you from falling into fear.

- Assess your savings and equity. That's what they're there for. Figure out how long you can float.
- Define what frightens you most. Is it money? Not having a position in a company? Feeling humiliated?
- Be honest about how willing you are to ask for financial or emotional help.

If you're clear on how long you can ride out unemployment, know the roots of your fears, and are willing to ask for help when you need it, you will be able to weather and even enjoy the pause in your working life. If you have real issues with money (and I mean *real* issues), then you have survival concerns and must find work. And you will. If you have problems with losing your title or the humiliation of being let go, check out the Instructions for self-esteem in Part III. If you are not willing to ask for help when you need it, you can be sure the universe will grind you down to a level where you have to ask. It's back to "You get what you resist."

Lull Is Good

Look for employment but enjoy the lull as much as you can. You'll find another job and make more money and feel all that particular stress again, I promise. But if you let your fear, anxiety, or shame take over the whole gift of time, you'll be even more stressed than you were when you had a job. My friends have used their unemployed times to lose weight, exercise, spend time with their family, reconnect with old friends, write a story or book, join a choir, volunteer—there are so many things to do when you have the time. Just sitting at a café at two o'clock in the afternoon can be an amazing experience. Enjoy it while you can.

Instructions for Employment

Endings and cycles are inevitable in nature and in your life, boom and bust and everything in between. You'll have more productive years and less productive. You'll feel creatively hot and then cool. It's normal. Discontent arises most often when you try to sustain a high when it's clearly time for a plateau or a dip. Every year cannot be a great year. Look back and plot good years and lean years throughout your life. Get to know your own cycle.

When you feel that bumpy times are ahead, bend your knees a bit, the way you do when standing on a bumpy bus. Keep your psychological and emotional knees bent so that if you do get jostled, you can sustain the impact. Even in a thriving career, keeping your knees bent emotionally is a way to keep that energy loose so that your fists don't clench.

THREE INSTRUCTIONS
FOR UNEMPLOYMENT DISCONTENT

Instruction 1: Don't make the myth true.
❧ Myth: It's easier to get a job while you're in a job. That's only true if you let your power dim because you lost a job. You can get any job you want if you put your power forward and your fear on the side. Discontent in the form of low self-esteem, neediness, or "rustiness" can permeate your interviews and by default make that myth true. But it doesn't have to be the case.

Instruction 2: Keep open to redirection.
❧ If doors keep closing on you, you're being redirected. Go for jobs that you want and don't worry about your qualifications. Take chances. Disrupt your rhythm and abandon assumptions.

Employment

Breaking out of your narrow view of what is possible will only open more doors and land you in a better place. Do what you really want to do with your life. Here's your chance. See "Career Changes" on page 58.

Instruction 3: Take your power to the interview.
➤ Before going to an interview, visualize yourself with your full and shining power surrounding you. Feel your hands and make sure they're relaxed. Know that if this job is right, you will get it. Breathe that knowledge into your heart. When you feel that's true, you can get up and go. You need to find the right fit, and anything that doesn't feel right, isn't.

Trust and faith hold some keys to reemployment as well. Put your faith in the universe. Pray, meditate, *allow*. Ask for help from your spiritual connection. It will come. Seek support from your friends and family when you need it. You'll end up with pearls of unexpected wisdom and some laughs, too.

Hitting the Bottom and the Two-Week Rule

A year ago a friend of mine was laid off. She used the first few months of her unemployment to shake off the stress of her last job. When she began her job search, she found it difficult. Not much was available at her level, she didn't get much encouragement from recruiters, and there was little opportunity to try something different. She sunk a little bit into discontent but managed to cope. Finally, after about four months of looking and seeing nothing of promise in her future, she felt the cold grip of discontent and wondered if she'd ever work again. My sister, who had been unemployed a few times in the past, told her that experience had proven a "two-week rule." If she had now sunk to that dreadful, fearful low where she was about to give up, she'd probably get a job in two weeks. She did.

When you get to what you think is your nadir, you're usually at your turning point. Surrender to your circumstances and somehow

57

you will end up just fine. I believe strongly in that state of grace, and I hope you do, too. If you ever get there, you'll know what I mean.

My sister Carol recently experienced this. She was laid off from her strategic-planning job in an industry downturn. Few jobs were available over the months, and though she interviewed, none materialized. Eventually her savings were depleted and her expenses amounted to more than her unemployment check. She felt powerless and scared, but she knew that she was doing everything she could, so she just let go. Whatever was going to happen would happen. The next day she got a call for freelance work and was working—at a very fair rate—by the following week. No more money troubles—for now.

Divine intervention. It happens.

Career Changes

Discontent from unemployment or the wrong employment can have you wishing you were doing something else. I strongly encourage you to think about pursuing a career that makes you happy. That's part of being abundant and powerful.

The right career can make any salary seem "enough." You'll be rich with satisfaction, power, and fulfillment, and money usually follows.

INSTRUCTIONS FOR CAREER CHANGE

- *Take your time.*
- *Get it right.*

  ❧Many people know they are in the wrong career, but don't know how to find the right one. Take time to explore the directions you might want to take. Talk to people, take some classes, become familiar with the area you think interests you. You may change your mind as many times as you want. That's how you find what is right. You'll always come back to what intrigues you.

- *Avoid pressured deadlines.*
  ❧It's daunting to have to live up to an arbitrary deadline that you've created. Sure, deadlines for making changes help, especially if you're prone to procrastination. But they might also add to your discontent when you don't meet them. Career changes take their own time to sort out. You can't make them happen on *your* timetable.
- *Be honest—no cop-outs.*
  ❧Whatever career you choose to pursue, make sure it's right for you. You don't have to earn approval. I know some people who have dropped law to pursue yoga, and some social workers who have gone back to school for law degrees. I know people who love to administer high colonics and those who like to sell over the telephone. The only career that you should choose is the one that makes you happy.
- *Give it time.*
  ❧Large-scale change takes considerable time. Be prepared to work in transition positions where you can make money to support the demands of your life, but still give way to time and opportunity to move into a new career. Abandon any career change that you think should or will happen quickly—because it won't.

I was in advertising for thirteen years, nine of which were steeped in career discontent. I spent eight of those nine years casting about, researching different ideas for work, including fundraising, marketing for nonprofits, and television development. I didn't even think of writing until the end of those nine long years. Researching what I wanted to do took time, as did finally getting down to what my next step would be and having the courage to do it. I needed all of that time to get there. Hopefully your career shift won't take so long, but if it does, remember, you'll get there when the time is right.

Health

WHEN my daughter was born, my husband was just finishing a postdoctoral fellowship and was about to start a search for his first academic job. His pay was barely enough to support the two of us and our little baby, and with an infant, it was impossible for me to earn money writing or doing astrological charts. My husband's parents had given us some money for a down payment on an apartment, but we couldn't buy one because we didn't know what city we were going to live in (no one would have given us a mortgage at the time anyway). It was fallback capital we didn't want to touch.

Our daughter was born near the winter solstice and was colicky on and off from midnight to 6 A.M. from the age of three weeks to three months. She screamed for hours night after winter night and slept just enough during the day to let me do the dishes, shop at the grocery store, and take a shower between writing thank-you notes for baby presents. We never slept. My husband ran to work in the morning grateful to be away from us. We lived in a small one-bedroom apartment and it was impossible to escape.

I sat, night after night, with my screaming daughter on my shoulder, on my lap, swaying and singing and doing what I could. I would watch the clock tick past 4, 5, 6 A.M. By seven, I would turn on the *Today* show and start the morning feeding. I used to watch Katie Couric and think, how could she be so lucky? She has two great children, a nice husband, a well-paying job, and meets so many great people. Why does she get so much and we get so little? Then, a few weeks later, her husband died.

I was shocked. I didn't know that he'd been ill, and all of a sudden, this icon of womanhood who "had it all" was tossed off the pedestal of perfection I'd put her on.

Katie's life suddenly didn't look ideal anymore. I was comfortable with our life, we were healthy, and our daughter had the strongest set of lungs on the planet. I stopped looking at others enviously and started taking stock of my own assets. There were plenty of them. I was grateful for the many blessings we did have, and I was able to feel compassion again. Although we were going through a hard time, it wasn't about loss, it was about life.

Your Most Valuable Asset

It's folly to mention prosperity and not mention the one and only asset you absolutely have to have: your health. If you're sick or physically challenged, you might have more than discontent on your hands. Feeling sick—just a sore throat or a bad cough—can make you remember how awful it is not to have a body in good, working order. If you're chronically ill, if you're facing serious disease, you may be facing survival issues. Rather than diagnosing discontent, you might find it more helpful to read inspirational stories or hear from experts about ways to make your spirit rise to the occasion.

I bring up physical health because discontent can bring on bad health, and bad health can cause discontent.

I'm not a doctor but I do know the value of listening to those you trust who do understand your health. Ignoring your health is just another form of denial that will bury you one way or another.

If you're discontented and you notice that your health is poor, your first step toward dissolving your discontent is to deal with your body. Even minor indigestion can be a sign of the root of your discontent.

Symbolism in the Symptoms

Every part of your body and every function within has a metaphorical significance in your life. In mind-body-spirit connection, each physical malady has an emotional and intellectual counterpart.

Health

Here are some common locations for discomfort and what problems they symbolize.

BODY PART	PROBLEM
Headache	Contained energy or stress
Neck	Shouldering burdens
Heart	Forgiveness issues
Digestive tract	Assimilation problems
Hips/lower back	Balancing
Knees	Problems with authority
Legs/feet	Being too distracted or too busy

Little Ills Have Large Impact

Certain discomforts that your body experiences can be both a symptom of your discontent and an aggravating factor. Feeling normal but lousy taints your life and puts you into a funk that amplifies whatever's bugging you.

I'm talking about constipation, gas, PMS, chronic headaches or other pain, and fatigue. They might not be appetizing subject matter, but neither is discontent. If you have any of these problems chronically, you are constantly reducing your available physical energy and probably your emotional and creative health. It's uncomfortable! When you're compromised physically, you will most likely feel discontent more acutely.

Don't Swallow Everything You're Given

If you watch TV, you'll know that medications for constipation and gas are everywhere. In the mind-body-spirit connection, your physical circumstances can indicate something on a deeper level. The process of eating and digesting is like taking in an idea and comprehending it. Your body takes in food and takes what it needs and tosses off the rest. If you get stuck, as in constipation, you have a lot of waste stuck inside you. What are you having a hard time releasing in your life? What else won't move? Are you having problems assimilating something in your life? If you have gas, your body is reacting to something you put into it. It's having a hard time getting it into your system. Are you having a hard time taking in what someone else is handing you? Are you being asked to swallow something that doesn't agree with you? Do you want to blow off some steam?

These are simplified metaphors for bigger problems in your life, but just considering them can help dissolve the blockage and its accompanying discontent. Your stress level can easily bring on physical reactions. And be honest with yourself emotionally as well as nutritionally. If all that cheese or hot sauce isn't working for you, find something that does.

Don't self-medicate these conditions if you experience them often. Your physical health is too important to constantly treat with easy fixes unless a doctor tells you to.

This isn't to say that your condition won't go away with a prescribed laxative or a good dose of antacid, but it will return if there's a deeper, underlying issue.

So *What* If It's That Time of the Month?

PMS is hard to resolve. There are natural therapies, herbs, and vitamins that can relieve some symptoms, but by and large if you have it, it doesn't go away easily. Be aware that PMS is a disequilibrium caused by various hormone levels coming and going like the tide. PMS can make you feel down, crabby, or just rotten. It is transient, but unlike constipation or gas, it can return even if you are in balance in every part of your life. With that in mind, try to go easy on yourself and others when you're suffering from PMS. You're going to feel everything, even your discontent, more acutely. It's probably not the time to make a big grandstand about what's bugging you because you may be more emotional or get angrier than you need to. You're not going to feel the same way in a matter of days. Sure, there's discontent there, but when your body's out of whack, you might want to wait until your PMS dissolves before you take an ax to it. There is such a thing as peaceful resolution.

Who Says "It Hurts So Good"?

I hurt my back while writing this book. I picked up my daughter from an awkward position and strained a muscle. I found a chiropractor who helped me and diagnosed my back as a "rib out." I can attest that having back pain is enough to make anyone unhappy until it stops.

Not all pains and aches can easily be treated or diminished. Some people live with pain every day. It is its own kind of discontent.

You have no choice but to cope with your pain in every way that you have available: over-the-counter medications, chiropractors, medical doctors, acupuncture, hands-on healers, meditations. Many resources might help. If you don't find any relief, you have a permanent layer of difficulty added to your life, to your discontent.

I know brave people who carry on normal lives in spite of continual pain. That is enormously courageous. It takes great energy and focus to deal with chronic pain. To live a life with pain, you need to make peace with it, not resist it. Allow your life to carry on with this unfriendly companion; open up the space within yourself to just be with it. Once you allow for your pain to be present, it won't hurt as much; you won't be pushing against it with your mind or heart, so you'll have both free to pursue more of your life.

Having pain is a spiritual experience, a wake-up call. It shows you—and others around you—how fragile your body can be. It reminds you how great it is to feel normal. Pain teaches tolerance and spaciousness. It is an exercise in faith, trust, and endurance.

Too Tired to Deal

If you're tired, the world is going to be less bright to you. If you're sleepy, you're going to miss a lot of details in your life and your family's life. Will you hear and see all that your child presents to you? Will you notice hints for more attention or indirect requests for affection? And when you're tired, you're going to be crabby. Even though you might experience some ups, any little down will take you right back to discontent—even if your life is going okay. Being tired magnifies sadness, anger, and a sense of helplessness. If you don't have any energy, you're not going to feel you can do anything productive. At least 63 percent of Americans don't get the recommended eight hours of sleep per night. We have a growing sleep deficit, and this is not something to brag about. The art of the siesta is dying out all over the world. No wonder everyone has such a short temper.

The National Sleep Foundation says lack of sleep causes irritability and can lead to serious accidents. Sleep deprivation over time can also lead to mood disorders such as depression.

I saw this in my father. He was depressed for many years. He also snored so much it kept most of our household awake. When, after years of problems, he finally mentioned his sleep problems to a doctor, he found the cause: sleep apnea. He couldn't breathe deeply or consistently enough during the night to sustain REM sleep (that's when you dream). His doctor informed him that without REM sleep, you get depressed. After he was prescribed an apparatus to help him breathe, my father became a different person. He was much more alert. He remembered details about our lives we didn't expect him to know. He laughed and enjoyed life much more. He had needed to sleep and to dream, and when he did, it changed his life. Dreaming isn't a waste of time, it's a healing process.

Enough Said?

Are you still discontent? Even though you know that your prosperity surrounds you every day? And that you have what you need—and can even get things that you want? Chances are your discontent is settling into what you think are prosperity problems, but it's more than likely from another part of your life. Prosperity gets a lot of anxiety because you think that money is going to make you happy, but it's probably not about money.

Are you happy in love? With your family and friends? Do you feel comfortable with the people in your life? Read on. Part II will address a whole other big topic—and while you can't live on love, you don't want to live without it.

Your Own Instructions

Your Own Instructions

Part II

Relationships

Relationships are unavoidable. And they are a source of infinite joy and discontent. We want to be loved but at times feel a lack of it. We want to be accepted without conditions. We want true love but haven't found the right person yet. We had true love and then we lost it. We want our friends and family to stand by us. We want everyone to tell the truth and act with integrity.

Love and its partner, like, are serious matters for feelings so pleasurable, and emotional matters are perhaps the hardest kind of discontent to wrestle with, because no amount of logic can make you feel any better. It's all about trust, faith, and having the courage to feel vulnerable. Gulp.

The key to the discontent of love is that it simply isn't going to be handled in ways you will necessarily understand or embrace. It's an easy place for a skeptic to get annoyed and give up. But then, love isn't something that you can really define or formulate. The essence of love's magic is also its most troublesome quality: it can't be controlled by you or anyone else.

Up to this point I've led you to believe that discontent can be managed (it can) and even resolved (also possible). But in the discontent of love, you have to get loose and be ready to try new methods to melt into happiness.

As far as emotions go, I consider love best of all. Joy is a great companion to love, and in a way, love is a type of concentrated personal joy being directed toward someone else. Joy isn't always about love, nor is joy as personal.

Jesus preached love and forgiveness, which both have remarkable healing qualities and can make almost any situation tolerable. Love and forgiveness have magical powers when they are real, authentic, open, and unrestricted.

Love and forgiveness are spiritual teachings because they are hard to practice every day and in every way. It's not human nature to love and forgive in flowing generosity. Quite the contrary: we are more likely to judge, step back, and wonder if love is "deserved," forgiveness "earned."

Love, both romantic and nonromantic, demands a great deal of consideration in a book about discontent. My astrology clients want to know about love right after, or even before, their prospects for prosperity. Relationships are mysterious and confounding, and love offers us a lifetime of challenge and entertainment. Whether in romantic love or with family and friends, you're never really finished dealing with people.

In discontented relationships, you can diagnose issues based on the three threads of change: karma, power, and fear.

Karma in Relationships

Karma can be used to explain both good relationships ("I must have been good to deserve this great mate") and, perhaps more usefully, bad ones ("I must have been awful to this guy in another life because he's making me miserable").

You certainly don't have to know about karma or believe in it to dissolve the discontent around love issues, but you might find it useful when you ask yourself "Why me?" or "How did this monster get to be my brother?" or "Why do I keep getting control-freak bosses?" The law of karma is an excellent way of understanding why you're hanging out with all your people (family, friends, and lovers) and what you can learn from them. These people are in your life for a reason, and you are all supposed to learn from each other. That's not necessarily a happy experience, but it *can* be. At a minimum, karma serves as a handy scapegoat when you find yourself at a loss for why people do the things they do.

Karma works differently for family, friends, and romance, precisely because you have different issues with each of these relationship sectors. Family issues have taken over our consciousness for the last twenty years as talk shows and books have encouraged us to "stop the chains of abuse" and to scrutinize our family relationships to make sure they function properly. Dysfunctional family relationships are certainly karmic, and the way to heal them (and dissolve this karmic tie) is to stop participating in the dysfunction. Easier said than done.

Friendships are different in that they are more your choice, so you're less likely to see karma right away. Sometimes it's good karma, by the way, but often your friends can serve up some pretty hefty lessons to you even though they are your most supportive system of relationships. Friendship karma is probably the last thing on your plate, after sorting out family and romantic love. But watch out—it's there.

And now, true love. What can karma do about it? Karma brings you a parade of possible partners. Choose from a delightful selection of your favorite past-life acquaintances. Mind you, my husband, a scientist, sniffs at this and considers it a kooky fallback position for people who have a hard time finding love, but he married me, didn't he? I've seen karmic marriages (I'm in one) and even karmic divorces. I've had clients who've told me about their first marriage and now wonder why they ever married that person. They even have kids together but now have nothing at all left in common. That's karma for you. You don't have to know why you were drawn together, but you can learn from it and work with it and not have to do something like that again. And those kids are usually a good enough reason to have been together in the first place—talk about karmic teachers!

Karma is one component in understanding relationship discontent; your karma sets up the kind of discontent you need to evolve from—even if you don't understand it at the time or see it in action.

Power—a Relationship Subtext

Defined as the influence you have over outcomes and choices, power is an important component in relationship discontent: who has it and who doesn't. In every relationship there's an unspoken agreement of "who has the power." When you're born, your parents have it all. With the onset of speech, you begin to acquire some. By the time you're an adult, you have your own power and share it with your parents, as clearheaded, mature people do. This happens far less often than we hope.

Power is a big deal in ongoing relationships, both romantic and platonic. Whom do you listen to? Who has the last word? Who holds the various outcomes to trials of life in their hands? These are all power issues. Power is what you use to give and take, compromise and forgive. Power in a healthy relationship is shared and respected. It shifts back and forth and grows between you. Feeling powerless or threatened by another's power is what brings on those buckets of discontent.

Fear

Here's where things get a little sticky. All of us confront fear in every relationship we have. We fear our children will be sick or hurt. We fear our friends will abandon us. We fear our love relationships will turn on us or die. You don't need to be a fully vested neurotic to face these fears every day, but they live somewhere between our unconscious and our conscious lives, giving us bad moments, bad dreams, and bad behavior.

Fear can really mess up a good relationship. You could be treating your loved ones badly or get treated badly because someone is ruled by fear. Acting out of fear can destroy many essential components in your relationship, such as trust, fidelity, and honesty. Fear makes you want to prevent something from happening. It can make you want to hide from reality, and worse, fear can distort reality and lead you to act rashly.

I know a woman in her early fifties who was afraid her husband was going to leave her for a younger woman. Acting out of her fear of abandonment, she started an affair of her own, hoping she'd have a fallback relationship. Her husband found out about her affair and her marriage fell apart. Her affair ended after her marriage fell apart. Her husband ended up remarrying a woman in her fifties. Acting out of fear brought this woman exactly what she feared most—being alone. Ironically, her fears of younger women were unfounded.

You always have to check your fear quotient when immersed in love discontent. You might just be your own worst enemy. Power issues trigger fear. Karmic issues spur on power plays and prey on fears. You get where I'm going? It's an integrated threesome that plays havoc with our relationships.

Love Credentials

Before launching into these tantalizing, ever-present discontents, however, I will give "full disclosure" of my "credentials."

My experience with romantic love and its varying discontents isn't from the sidelines. I longed to date as a teenager but wasn't exactly overwhelmed with calls. I had serious relationships in college and throughout my twenties and early thirties, but none was "the one." After a few stinging breakups, I found an excellent therapist who helped me untangle my beliefs and bad habits so that I came to understand much more about discontent in love. Just having decided to be single for life, I met my husband and married him when I was thirty-six. As an author of three other books dealing with love, I have interviewed people, explored issues, and discussed love problems for many years. As an astrologer, I've seen love issues in many guises, and I know that love problems are not age- or gender-sensitive. I've witnessed love succeed in its many forms. And I've seen love's failures in multitissue losses.

Your best love lessons will evolve from your own experiences. Discontents with family and friends are pretty common, and solutions are not terribly tricky, but you have to be flexible.

It's all up to you. That's the truth.

Romantic Love

ROMANTIC love is at its core a three-act grand opera:

1. The Search for True Love
2. Keeping the Flame Alive
3. Healing When Love Leaves

Most love discussions, at least among women, are about finding love. Once found, love must be guided gently to keep it on course. If step 2 isn't properly attended to, step 3 will happen. Of course, one can still vigilantly obey step 2 but still encounter step 3. That's what makes love so fearfully difficult: it's not a sure thing. Love is not practical. You can't sue someone for not loving you. But that doesn't mean you can't learn how to play with it skillfully. Instructions do help love discontent.

For many, the pursuit of romantic love is the most important pastime of life, then, once love is found, it's the most neglected.

All the energy is in the chase. Naturally, the path to finding the right partner is mysterious, but making a relationship work is no less challenging. But, first things first.

The Chase

Love confounds us because we try to apply all of our logic to getting what we want, and no rational method will help. If someone gives you a formula for finding love, you can certainly try it, but don't be frustrated if it doesn't work. It's like a fad diet: you hear it really works, but you find you can't fulfill the demands of the regimen.

Instructions for Your Discontent

I've come to understand that the way to attract romantic love is simple, so get settled and be ready to be treated like a child.

Sally: A Story of Love Infertility

SALLY: I'm open. I joined a gym. I work out. I go to mixers at my church. I tried a dating service. I don't have a type, or limits, or even an age requirement. I would even use The Rules if I could find someone to use them on.

ME: And?

SALLY: Nothing! It's all such a waste. I'm doing everything. I even bought high heels and had my makeup done and now I have this consultant that helps me pick the most flattering clothes. And still nothing. I considered going to Paris this summer and flying business class to increase my chances of finding a guy with a good job.

ME: What stopped you from going?

SALLY: I didn't want to go to Paris alone.

ME: So what's the problem?

SALLY: I'm not meeting anybody.

ME: You mean you go out and to these mixers and meet men with this service but you still don't meet them?

SALLY: You know what I mean. I haven't met "the one."

ME: How long have you been doing this?

SALLY: Over a year. And the year before that I was getting over my divorce and the years before that I was married to the wrong guy. I can't take it anymore. I'm never going to find someone. What should I do?

ME: Quit.

SALLY: Huh?

ME: You heard me. Quit. What's the point? It's not working. Just quit doing all that stuff and forget about it. You won't find love. You're going to be alone the rest of your life. (*I'm laughing.*)

SALLY: What are you, some sort of sicko? Why are you laughing at me? I'm in pain. I'm thinking of taking Prozac.

Maybe I'll feel better and then maybe I'll meet someone. Look at my chart. Am I depressed?

ME: *(Laughing harder.)* I'm not laughing at you. I'm laughing
with you.

SALLY: But I'm not laughing.

ME: Yeah. That's what's missing.

SALLY: Huh?

ME: How about a sense of humor? How about being able to
laugh at yourself?

SALLY: Why should I? It's not funny. I'm not a joke.

ME: Okay, let me explain.

In our search for love and our desire to be amazed by love, we
often lose our sense of humor. It's a classic mistake. Finding love
requires being lovable—which requires smiling, enjoying yourself,
and generally being relaxed. This, my friends, is the trick.

Love Infertility

Being "love fertile" depends on a number of variables that you
must assess with objectivity. Most love infertiles lie to themselves
(I know I did). I suggest asking a friend to go over the list with you.
That way you won't be able to avoid the truth about yourself.

Here are some things that keep love from landing:

QUALITIES THAT PROMOTE LOVE INFERTILITY

- *Looking for it.*
  ❧Love likes to surprise. If you are always on the alert, it
  won't be able to leap out and change your life.
- *Absenteeism.*
  ❧Having to move around or travel constantly is a handy way
  to foil love. When a nice opportunity occurs, too often we
  abandon love's fertile grounds to be somewhere else. I hear
  this one all the time, especially from busy professionals who
  need to keep moving to keep that feeling of making progress,

of "getting somewhere." They don't have time to feel lonely. I know: I used to be a member of that club.

- *Fear of being hurt.*

 ❧We all have this one. No one wants to hand her heart to another only to have it handed back in bite-sized pieces. But you have to take a risk if you want to be in love, so get used to little steps instead of leaping off cliffs. Love is exciting enough without extreme actions.

- *Need to please the parents.*

 ❧Believe it or not, an epidemic of parent-pleasing is going on. Even without a religious dictate, a tiny part of you wants to find the person you think your parents want for you. The need for approval is getting in the way of your desire for love. Now grow up.

- *The best one got away.*

 ❧No, he didn't, but you're still stuck on someone in your past who has you in love-lock. It is important to get over everyone you've ever dated so that you are free to fall for someone else.

- *Staying with the wrong one until you find the right one.*

 ❧Many people easily succumb to the notion that it's better to be in any relationship than no relationship. *Mais, non!* I say. You are fooling yourself! Being unavailable immediately narrows your field. Even if you tell yourself you're "technically" available (we don't have sex, we have an understanding that we see other people), you're not really free to develop a true love relationship. You'll get involved only with people who don't mind that you're not free—it's a sticky relationship energy you form with them. Rest assured that holding on to what amounts to a dead body is not attractive.

- *Meeting the right one at the wrong time.*

 ❧Related to "the one that got away," this platitude is utter nonsense. For true love to grow, you can't think that you had only one chance and you blew it. This kind of energy forces you to settle down with someone who is only second best. And that's a recipe for failure.

- *They are either gay or taken.*

 ❧What hooey. This is the coward's way out. You can say it,

you can mean it, and the world will respond to you in kind. But it's not true. I have seen love bloom at all ages and for all kinds of people. Hiding behind the "gay or taken" theme just makes you bitter—and that's truly unlovable.

- *Waiting.*

  ❧Here is the trickiest quality of all. You are not supposed to wait mindfully for your soul mate. You're meant to be open, available, unafraid, and ready, but you can't *wait*. The universe is more or less asking you to strike a pose of being perfectly happy, comfortable, and fulfilled while you're absentmindedly loitering for true love to clonk you on the head. You can't pretend you're not waiting; you really have to stop waiting. But how do you do that, if you're waiting for true love?

- *No sense of humor.*

  ❧This is deadly. You'll want to be able to laugh together as you ease into old age.

- *Prolonged drought.*

  ❧If you've been without a date or a decent opportunity for a date for some time—say more than three months—you may be enduring drought conditions. I've been there. Sometimes it's a healing experience, sometimes it's self-imposed, a time-out from your personal life. Whatever the cause, you've got to get out of it. To end the drought, you might need to do something outside the ordinary. Force yourself. Ask someone out. Try personal ads. Ask someone to set you up. *Do this as a ritual.* This isn't looking for love, it's looking for a renewed social life. Ask someone out whom you don't necessarily want to date more than once. It's a way of shaking yourself out of inertia, and it breaks the plain of nothingness in your love life. This is not to say that the person you'll meet is going to be a loser, but you need to end the drought by going out with anyone who qualifies as a date. Your personal energy will shift as a result, and you'll find that dating won't be such a mysterious world. Once you've broken through the drought, more opportunities will come to you.

- *Preferring fantasy to fact.*

  ❧To have a real relationship, you have to live in the real world.

ROMANTIC LOVE RE-BELIEF

🌤 *Romance is play, not work.*

To promote your love fertility, you'll need a wide-open space, a playground, and a soft green hill to play on. You need to realize that the whole world is your space, where you can meet the right love partner. You don't have to qualify your world as only "work, friends, gym, and church." You might meet someone at a stoplight, a restaurant, or a train station. You also have to be playful, not practical. Even if you do meet a wonderful new person, you can get bogged down (and be boring) in details about life, such as asking "Where do you work?" or "Who do you know?" instead of using your surroundings just to flirt. Be playful on that playground. And that soft green hill is a great place just to hang out and relax together, to take a breather and to get to know each other. Let's see if we can go back to childhood so that you can remember how to play again.

Children are always open to making new friends. Little kids don't overanalyze this part of life. You need to remember this when you're looking for love. A child might be shy or afraid of a new playmate at first, but he will find a way to get along. A child might want to be friends but still take time to establish closeness, playing nearby to allow time and nature to edge friendship closer.

As an adult, you don't talk to strangers without a reason or without a healthy suspicion; you don't think people are really as good as they seem, and you don't take stupid chances (or at least chances you think are stupid). This makes it difficult for you to keep playful, and the playground can start to look like a place to make a fool of yourself or take a fall and get hurt.

When you try out the following Instructions, find the kid in you who wants to have a great time.

Love Fertility Instructions

1. Be open to making new friends.
2. Play just for fun, not for keeps.
3. Take a rest period—you can always get up and play again.

INSTRUCTION #1: BE OPEN

❧ You need to be open to everyone as a *potential* new playmate, not as a prospective coparent. You need to relax and see what happens (this is the soft green hill).

- *Minimize emotional barriers.*

   ❧ You're probably already putting up emotional barriers and fences that keep your playground too small. I know I did. For me, it was the "right profession." (I dared to declare I'd never marry a doctor. Guess what I did?) For some people, it's the right college degree, religion, race, country of origin, to name a few common fences. You might not even know you're doing it.

- *Resist screening or profiling.*

   ❧ If you've ever gone on a blind date, you know what I mean. Someone calls you and asks if you're interested in meeting a friend of his or hers. You say, "What's he/she like?" as your radar zooms in: Will this person be allowed in? I used to use the game "If he were a celebrity, who would he be?"—which was a good way to diminish the person before he even rang up for a date. Your friend compares your prospective date to someone desirable like Prince William or Brad Pitt, and the poor man can never live up to the image. Disappointment meets you at your door.

In retrospect, I see how terribly love infertile I was in my twenties, and I paid for it by meeting only the guys who sounded good on paper. One was insufferably dull, full of himself and his self-ascribed intellectual standing. I feigned interest in long-winded stories about other people I had never heard of (but they wrote for

The New Yorker!) and I never questioned why I was doing it. Another guy I dated was unstable, overcritical, always comparing himself with other men, so I became his (unpaid) therapist. Bad move. Yet another boyfriend was just too distant and he never really let me get to know him. I passed on anyone who didn't fit my criteria, and later, when I learned more about relationships from my examining them in therapy, I was able to meet men who were more love fertile, too.

When I met the man who became my husband, I wanted to dismiss him right away—sinking into love infertility. I gave him a hard time. First, I demanded to see his driver's license (I thought he was under twenty-one; he was thirty). I lectured him on spirituality, and because he was born in Austria, I interrogated him about his family's activities during World War II. I didn't believe him when he told me he was a scientist, and when I found out it was true, I told him how much I hated science.

Even though I was being very love infertile, he was patient and I resisted the temptation to shoot him down for good. I was having fun!

On our second date and after many e-mails, we sat in a dark café in a seedy section of New York's East Village. It was long after sunset on a summer night and still an insufferable ninety-five degrees. We were drinking gin and tonics and sweating. I was lecturing about UFOs or some other topic that he thought was funny, and he turned to me, one eyebrow raised. I stopped talking after a minute and he asked, "How can someone so beautiful be so full of nonsense?" To which I responded, "Oh, I suppose you think just because I have big brown eyes I'm this sweet little—"

He cut me off. "Oh, you're not sweet." At which point I began to fall in love.

This guy was willing to tell me the truth about myself and he was in relentless pursuit. We were playing a kind of emotional tag and just then he "got" me. This was what I had always hoped for: someone who would see me for who I was, tease me, know my foibles, and still love me. I could be myself—even my silliest, weirdest self—and be loved. I could also be my best self, and that is what love inspired, because of his faith in me. Thank goodness the clouds parted and I was able to see clearly that I should give this guy a chance.

Soon after this conversation I had a discussion with my therapist, still resisting letting him get closer:

ME: He's not my type.

SL: What do you mean?

ME: You know, he's not my type. He's too young, he's not American, he's not Jewish, and for chrissakes he's a scientist.

SL: And what is your type?

ME: Not that.

SL: I think that if you think he's not your type, he's going to be good for you.

ME: How's that?

SL: Have you ever dated "your type"?

ME: Sure.

SL: Are you happy? Are you satisfied? Are you married?

ME: Point taken.

I share this with you so that you can see that I had to learn the same thing you should: don't use stupid rules you have made up about the "right" kind of person for you. You're going to be wrong.

I also get asked all the time, "What's the right astrological sign for me?"

There's no answer for that. Even the most unsuitable astrological matches can work. You just don't know. That's why you need to stay open and work against who you think your spouse should be, what you think your parents want, and whom you think your friends expect. You have to believe that you're not the odd man out on Noah's ark. You have a mate out there, a partner who's getting ready for you. You haven't yet met, so make room for "the right one" in your heart by letting go of the idea that everyone good is already involved, you're too old, or the right one got away. You don't really want to believe it anyway; that's just what you tell yourself when you're sad or lonely or pissed or grumpy: discontented. Make room in your hopes that the right one is out there. That little wedge of wishing will change your energy so that magic—Cupid's arrow—can take aim and find its target.

INSTRUCTION #2: PLAY FOR FUN

✎If you're dating and meeting people who might just turn out right for you, you have to get to know them first. You must play. No one seems to remember this part.

- *Don't play casting agent.*

✎You might get impatient for love, as if you're casting for a romantic lead in a new movie and you're getting way too many hopefuls.

You might just start sounding like a Hollywood cliché: "Don't call us, we'll call you." You think this is fun? It's work, dammit. It's not about the fun.

Love infertility soars when you make dating an audition for true love. Even if the poor soul who was meant to be your mate is right in front of you, you could shuffle him along without really seeing him. Take heart: if he's meant to be your mate, he'll find his way back to you again, but it would be easier and certainly more courteous to allow every potential suitor a few minutes in your playground. See if they like jungle gyms, a game of tag, a little jump rope.

- *Don't be a wet blanket.*

✎You have to play, too. Here's where a sense of humor is so important. Be able to laugh. You don't have to laugh at the same things, but you must be able to enjoy yourself, make your own fun. That's a sign of being ready for love.

This isn't to say that every person you meet is someone you must play with, but if you're using a dating service, being set up by friends, or just get asked out a lot, make the most of it. Don't dis someone you think is boring if you haven't been fun yourself. And no fake fun, either. Don't pretend to enjoy yourself. Like cheating on a diet, you will only cheat yourself. Only the genuine stuff works.

- *Don't bail too early.*

  ❧ Playing fair is another matter. Try not to jump to conclusions too quickly ("She's perfect!" or "No way!") because you won't be giving a fair shot to anyone if you make an early judgment call. Take into account that first dates are pretty much meant to be transitions into second dates. You won't get much out of that first encounter other than chemical attraction (if your fear doesn't intrude) or surface compatibility. You don't get to know someone that quickly. So think about making it to a second date, and do what you need to make the first one as pleasant as possible. Relax and breathe through those first fears that arise. Ask questions, even if you feel silly. A first date is for exploring what you have in common. It's just a means to get to know someone. Don't take it further than that.

- *Don't suffer.*

  ❧ That said, if it's a really dismal date, bail—politely but firmly. I'm not asking you to endure something awful: a date should be enjoyable, not a labor of Hercules. Have a good time. If it's simply not possible to find common ground for fun, get out. Save yourself—and your date. Not everyone is meant to be your playmate.

INSTRUCTION #3: TIME-OUT

❧ The real test of compatibility isn't in what you do together, but in what you don't do. It's those unplanned moments that open the door to intimacy.

- *Know when to call a time-out.*

  ❧ If you do find a fun playmate, eventually you're going to want to take a break from the fun and games. Go for a walk. Hang out on the soft green hill. Instead of charging around, trying to find out if your new playmate likes museums, country music, your hometown, your friends and family, just sit down and do nothing. Playmates can become partners, but the beginning of a relationship needs some time for adjustment and connection. It's easier and probably more successful when you do this slowly and in private, without the world watching to see if you two have a future together.

- *Do nothing—the way you like to.*
  ✎The soft green hill can actually be a tender time. When we dated, my husband-to-be and I spent a great deal of time just walking around the streets of New York, stopping at bookstores, having a cup of coffee or a margarita or a street vendor's ice. We talked about our childhoods, our friends and enemies. We talked a lot about our families and how different our backgrounds were, and we eventually discovered how much we really agreed on things. We laughed and joked a lot. We fell in love doing nothing in particular. You'll have your own "nothing," and it's a great thing to share.

- *Don't forget to laugh.*
  ✎The single most telling sign of falling in love is sharing your humor and developing your private jokes. The soft green hill is the best place to have a chuckle, giggle, or guffaw.

- *Nix on socializing.*
  ✎I've watched many people nip their relationships in the bud (or come close to it) by frantically arranging social engagements to show off their new playmate. It's certainly tempting—to get approval and to see everyone react to your new person. But there's plenty of time for that if you're really going to stay together.

  Socialize à deux and don't stack on the activities. The soft green hill is a place to rest, relax, and just be together without distractions. Try to resist playing tennis, seeing a movie, going bowling, and cooking dinner all in the same day. Your enthusiasm can be misinterpreted; your constant need for distraction can look like fear of being alone with your playmate.

- *Check your partner for signs of restlessness.*
  ✎If your partner can't sit still, you might want to tread carefully, too. Being with someone over the long term requires an attention span and a willingness to do nothing together. If you detect an unwillingness to do nothing with you, your playmate has some discontent or uncertainty. Proceed with caution.

- *Silence means it's serious.*

  ❧ If you are sitting on that soft green hill and just enjoying the view, you're sitting in a serious relationship. Doing nothing, saying nothing, and not noticing that it's nothing is a good sign for a good relationship.

The soft green hill requires stillness without distraction. When you're engaged in an activity, such as playing on the jungle gym, you can use a lot of tactics to keep yourself from being vulnerable. There's hide-and-seek, a game of tag, trying out stunts, or just clowning around. All of this is good fun, playing around the way you need to when you first meet a good playmate.

The resting part is difficult because all of these play tactics eventually get old. Dodging and role-playing are not going to get you very deeply in love. The soft green hill will take you deeper, but it requires the last step in love fertility: vulnerability, trust, allowing nature to take its course.

What Is Attractive? Not What You Think

AN ATTRACTION RE-BELIEF

❧ *Being vulnerable creates a natural magnetism. Your most fragile, inner self is the one that will attract the love you want.*

Being vulnerable is exactly what you want to avoid most of the time, isn't it? Who wants to be open to criticism, speculation, rejection? Yet being vulnerable is the key to forming that deep, lasting love bond you want in a partner. You have to show a little bit of it. It's a game of "I'll show you mine if you show me yours"—perfectly suitable to the soft green hill.

This isn't about getting physical, either, if you think that's where I'm going. No one should judge how fast or slow you take that part of your relationship, and the soft green hill can be a great make-out spot. But it's not a place to get naked. Engaging in physical relations, however far they may take you, can distract from true inti-

macy or can become another playground game. Real, loving connection, making love, is something you do consciously and purposefully, not to fill up time or space. It's commonly accepted that
first-date sex can be a long-term passion killer, but any sex too early
in a relationship can jeopardize your ability to adjust to emotional
depth; sex too early can (and often does) trigger a lot of fear, which
throws a cold, wet blanket over growing fires.

On the soft green hill, your focus should be about just being
together without an agenda. You have to let go and trust. Be yourself. Say something deep or stupid. Be funny or miss the mark. If
you're nervous, you can admit it. If you're feeling great, share
that energy—it's great karma. Be truthful and you lose nothing. Lie
or pretend and you don't have a real relationship anyway. There's
no trust when you don't allow yourself to tell the truth. One thing
helps you make this leap into vulnerability, and that's your humor.

Laugh in the Face of Fear

Back to Sally, my friend who lost her laughter. She had plenty of
dates (having a big playground wasn't her problem). She didn't
play much, though, because she evaluated the "worthiness" of
her prospects too early. And even if she met someone she thought
suitable, she would never have chanced a soft green hill. She
could not open herself to someone because she took everything so
seriously. Her fear stood between her and humor. This is where
she didn't let on that she loved herself—or even liked herself. She
couldn't be vulnerable enough to let love happen.

This is a big lesson for many of us (myself included). I learned
it over time, from friends who found humor in the things I found
embarrassing. Now I'm a lot less embarrassed about things than I
used to be. When you're fearful or defensive, being vulnerable
feels as if you're open to emotional annihilation. When you're
more secure, being vulnerable is simply letting someone look into
the window of your heart and see that you're human; that you
have fear, that you are real. Your own sense of humor is not for
self-deprecation but for showing that you're adorably imperfect.

Honesty has a way of disarming people. If they don't love what
they see, they'll respect it and treat you gently. If you meet someone who has disarming (and gentle) honesty, you'll probably be
compassionate with him or her.

Showing your playmate your vulnerability is not tantamount to
standing naked before a huge audience—this is no full monty. It's
a careful, cautious, step-by-step way to reveal the real you.

How Do You Know When It's Serious?

Let's say things are going well in a relationship. You're being open,
honest, and appropriately vulnerable. How do you know when it's
time to be serious? It will feel natural and you won't feel nervous
about bringing up the future. Yet you don't have to start talking
about your sister's wedding to bring up the subject of long-term
commitment. Your vulnerability will allow you to say, quietly and
humbly (as opposed to forcefully), "I'm looking forward to being
married one day. Are you?"

If you get a negative response, get up and find a better playmate.
If you get a "Yes, one day," keep going. While you're not setting a
date, you have an opening for establishing a deeper relationship.
Carry on. Play more, take more time out. When you feel you've
spent enough time together, you can decide whether this is a relationship headed for love. Chances are, if this is a solid relationship
on track for commitment, you won't have to ask.

Facts of Life

I know a few of you are wondering if you can find your soul mate
this way. There's one last caveat that no hopeful heart likes to
hear: your perfect partner is going to be flawed. No matter how perfect this person might seem to you, the poor soul is afflicted with as
many imperfections as you are—and has his own karmic path to
follow.

I know more than a few people who prefer to keep their fantasies alive and choose not to marry because of this. It's better for them, and it's their choice to make. If you are one of these people, no Instruction is going to help you realize your dreams. You'll have to cut the universe a little slack before you find the right one.

On Your Marks, Get Set, Go!

Now go off to the playground to see what playmates come your way. One tip: watch out for someone you're afraid of. If anyone makes you nervous (not in the way of trench-coat-wearing-stranger-trying-to-lure-you-into-a-car) because that person seems to really want to know you, you're probably headed for a karmic relationship and you're going to feel a lot of fear and attraction on and off for a while. Somewhere in your subconscious, you're going to know that this person is worth getting to know. So don't chicken out.

Dating Discontent

As you date, you're likely to encounter a great deal of discontent. While you're playing on someone's playground and taking time on the soft green hill, a certain amount of fear and power shifting is taking place. This can be navigated without touching on areas of discontent, but it's likely to set off at least one or two moments of uncertainty that can, if left unexamined, throw some cold water on your otherwise sunny, warm nature.

My girlfriends and I long ago defined dating as "seeing someone more than three times but without the understanding of exclusivity." Dating encompasses so many different approaches, from the traditional Saturday night dinner-and-a-movie to meeting at meditation class. You're the one (or two) who defines "dating"—how often you get together, how much romance, how much practicality—but it's all the same thing: time for two people to explore a friendship that may or may not lead to something passionate, serious, and committed. You can simply date for fun, without any intention of settling down or meeting a long-term mate. Cupid finds a mark whenever he feels like it. Dating isn't always just shopping for love, it's a place where you play, and once in a while you'll see your reflection in someone else's eyes, words, or gestures.

Discontent finds its way into dating because it's rejection roulette. Some "experts" will give you tips on minimizing how much you put yourself at the mercy of your date's wishes, but you won't be on a date in that case, you'll be on a manipulation. You can try to minimize feeling judged or rejected by using methods that supposedly "control" yourself to elicit the "right" reactions from your date, but they don't work, really. Don't follow anyone's rules for dating conduct if you're after a real, authentic, fun connection, even love. If you want to be liked and loved for *you*, you have to give up control and just let nature take its course.

Date Ratings

When you date, you open yourself up to someone else's approval-rating system. Are you smart enough? Cute? Fun? Thin? Successful? Savvy? Do you have that same sense of humor? Are you "cool"? Then there's also your internal critic, pointing out little bugaboos to keep you from taking emotional risks. Is your date living up to all of your ratings, too?

So many rating scales are in your head—and in everyone else's—that you're bound to get mired in self-doubt. All this because you're trying to get to know someone but you're *afraid* of the whole process.

What's to be afraid of? Rejection, embarrassment, humiliation? Yep. Rejection is really tough; who volunteers for getting cut loose? You don't want to feel bad about who you are or doubt your attractiveness. Don't be fooled by your friends who say they don't feel bad or weird about getting dumped or dissed. No one is immune from feeling rejected, but it doesn't have to ruin you. A little "Ouch!" once in a while tells you you're alive. It doesn't have to be discontent.

Dating is a seesaw of fear and power. Who calls whom, how

much you say or don't say, how much you let yourself care (or don't), how fast or how slow. Layers of signals and responses come with every date.

INSTRUCTIONS FOR DATING FEAR

- *Remember to breathe.*

  ✍I was a huge fear-mongering, stubbornly independent dater. I learned through hard work and good advice that breathing is essential to a good date.

  Are you thinking that I'm out of my mind? Before you pass judgment, think about how a first date feels. Are you holding your breath? Are you stiff? Sure you are. That's fear.

  If your palms are sweaty, or you're just having a hard time relaxing, you can't form complete sentences, you're in a fear state. Breathe. Take a deep breath into your body slowly through your nose. Exhale through your mouth. Repeat two times.

  Your deep breathing will calm you and allow you to collect yourself. Then you can carry on a conversation without falling apart.

  You will have a much better time with more oxygen in your system and you'll be a much better date than the gasping-for-air stranger who can't speak.

- *Breathe a night sky.*

  ✍Fear can also be released nicely during the evening with a soft inhalation of a night sky. Breathe the stars. If you don't believe in magic, you will when you breathe in the night air (with your mind's eye imagining starlight as part of the oxygen/nitrogen mix) and enjoy the intoxicating (but nonaddictive) effects of the stars' heavenly energy.

Noncommitters and "Potential"

It's a common mistake. You meet someone who is fantastic. This person has the same goals and dreams, the same humor and direction. You have a great time playing. You rest and relax together. But nothing more happens.

You can see the future. It's going to be so great!

But nothing more happens.

You get into a routine. You meet family, friends. You have an official, publicly established relationship, except for one thing: you don't talk about the future.

It's as if you have a gag order on the subject of your future. Holidays, vacations, birthdays come and go and are carefully low-key. Eventually, some marker of time will get to you. At a one-year anniversary or one Valentine's Day or the second birthday you spend together, you're waiting for that other shoe to drop. Whether it's the declaration of love or the official commitment words, they just don't appear.

You suck up more patience and wait. If you even broach the subject, somehow the mood sours or you get into a fight. Forget it, it's not time yet.

The brutal truth is that there will never be a good time for that discussion. I'm in favor of saying what you want to say, declaring what you need from a relationship as soon as you feel comfortable doing so. Why wait? If you got to this point of knowing you want a commitment, do you really have to put your needs on hold for this person who can't be pinned down?

No. The space you're giving to your beloved is only a stall tactic. You are either in love with potential or with a noncommitter, which amounts to the same thing. You don't see this person for his or her reality: you see what you want to see in the future.

I learned a valuable lesson when I once argued with a friend about a man I was seeing.

"He says he doesn't want a serious relationship right now, but I can tell he's really into me. He's probably just scared."

"What makes you think he's not telling you the truth?"

"I just know," I said, with great assurance.

He didn't want a relationship and he meant it. We stopped seeing each other a few weeks later.

What made me think that this guy wasn't being honest with me? Nothing, I simply wanted to believe my version of reality.

If you're grousing about dating someone for a long time and you're not getting what you want out of the relationship, you are wasting your time. You are stewing in your own self-made discontent.

INSTRUCTIONS FOR DATING NONCOMMITTERS AND POTENTIAL

- *Issue an ultimatum and be prepared to follow through. It is the only way to find out if you're waiting in vain.*

  ✎Ultimatum: "I want a commitment from you that we are going to be together for ————" (fill it in yourself).

  If you get what you want, you should be leaving Discontentville on the next train. If you don't: break up.

  It's time to move on. Take your power back and hit the road. Follow through on your ultimatum and you will feel the pain of separation and breakup, but you will have your life back. And your future is going to be a lot nicer with a person who loves you and makes a commitment to you. It's a bore and it hurts at first, but this step will free you from someone's undeveloped potential and ready you for someone who has evolved to your level.

Ultimatum Throwbacks

Often, but not in every situation, the ultimatum will be filed, the jerk will not step up, and you will be walking away with a heavy heart, when out of the blue you hear your name being called.

Walking away from the noncommitter can act like a shot of adrenaline and get the juices of "I can't lose you!" flowing. It doesn't happen every time, but if it does, you now have the power in your hands. You can make your demands (reasonable, please) and convert that noncommitter into a devoted partner. Go ahead as long as there is no counternegotiating or pullback when you get back together. No regressing into that waiting game again or your ultimatum has failed.

If your noncommitter did not rise off the sofa and come breathlessly running after you, good riddance. Go to the playground and find some fun.

Discontent in Date Breakups

My friend Joan just went through a date breakup. She had been under the impression that the guy she had been seeing was happy and that everything was going just swell.

J: That guy I like so much? He dumped me.
ME: What? Why? What happened?
J: Beats me. We'd been seeing each other for two months. We had such a great time. We'd just come back from a weekend at the beach and he didn't call me for two weeks. I e-mailed him and he didn't answer. I was pretty sure he was in town.
ME: That's weird.
J: Yeah. I figured I was getting dumped, so when he did decide to call me back, I didn't take his call or answer his e-mails.
ME: And that served what purpose?
J: I don't know. I just didn't feel like getting dumped. So then I finally called him back and he asked me to meet him at six-thirty for coffee.
ME: And that's bad?
J: That's bad. I just said, "What do you want to have coffee for at the end of the day? I don't want coffee. I'd rather go to the gym. What is it that you want to say to me?"
ME: Wow. That's direct.
J: Sure is. So he just said it.
ME: How'd he say it?

J: "I don't want to pursue this any longer."
ME: I guess that's clear. Any sign of why?
J: No, it's not like I got to poll the jury. I just said fine and hung up.
ME: Shred of dignity.
J: Shred? I'm wrapped in a large, pink pashmina of dignity.

Joan didn't let that guy see/hear/feel her reaction so that her dignity was left intact. Her belief, which I share, is that a date breakup doesn't merit any more than an "I see" reaction. Joan admitted to being hurt but got over it, as we all must, because he just wasn't the guy for her. That's the end of the story. You don't have to have a postgame show on a dating relationship. You might think you want one, but what's the point? You'll never know what the real reason is, just the convenient excuse you'll get to cover it:

No chemistry.
Not ready for a relationship.
Met someone else.
Got back with old boyfriend/girlfriend.
Can't handle extreme sports—*fill in the blank.*

The date was just a playmate who didn't want to play anymore. There's always someone else to play with (unless you want a breather, which is fine, too).

Dating discontent arises when you get disgusted from too many date breakups or when you just feel dispirited from not finding the right one. (See "Love Infertility" above and try a dating hiatus of ninety days. You need to reset your emotional availability, and a little rest is a perfect solution.) My friend Ann was tired of bozos. She has no shortage of opportunities to date, but a spate of men with bad manners and little to talk about put her off dating. Although she was continually asked out, she refused all dates for about three months. When it was time to "get back out there," she was ready. She found herself only accepting dates she genuinely wanted to go on, and so far, she's been enjoying them.

When you think your date is a source of discontent, the obvious solution is a date breakup. Why stick with someone who makes you unhappy? Your friends will be thrilled if you stop complaining. If you feel that you keep running into the same problem with different dating situations, you probably need a therapist. You might have some issues with intimacy or rejection that keep you from allowing a relationship to progress. You could also check out the section of this book about self-esteem. Many dating discontents are because we feel inadequate in some way. If you take time to do a little self-examination, you could figure out where your own little foibles are coming from.

Dating Karma

I have mentioned fear and power overwhelming a dating relationship, but not karma. The way to check out karma is in the breakup. If you've been in one of those intense emotional relationships where your date overwhelms you with compatibility and chemistry and then just gets over it and moves on, you've probably been mowed down by some karmic payback. Get up, dust yourself off, and move on. There's no telling where that karma came from, but you can be glad it's gone.

If you have a hard time getting over someone you met only briefly, it might not be karma as much as an imbalance in your self-esteem. Rejection isn't easy or pleasant, but it shouldn't plunge you into the depths of psychic hell for too long. If it does, you might just need to push your emotional "reset" button by taking time out and learning to play again. Find humor and you will find healing.

Existing Relationships
and Multitudes of Discontent

Let's say you've been dating someone for a while and you think you're embarking on a relationship. There is no magic formula for when dating stops and a "relationship" begins, but I subscribe to the ninety-day rule—after seeing someone for ninety days, you have a certified relationship.

Congratulations. You've made it through the playground and onto the soft green hill. Now you can go wherever you want. Now you can have relationship problems. And you will, of course, because relationships are always in play. There is no final score unless you split up.

I'm convinced that the finding of love becomes a memory in soft-focus candlelight after you've made your commitment. Your search has finished and you have the love of your dreams. Here's where karma, power, and fear take the stage to keep your relationship Fresh! Alive! Invigorating! (or) Intolerable! Stale! Suffocating!

It's hard to keep the glowing flame of new love burning. In fact, it's impossible. The universe pulls a big bait and switch. Sooner or later that prince or princess starts to test your tolerance and support.

While every relationship is different, couples do go through difficult periods, and individuals sometimes don't share their vulnerability, intimacy, and humor. Habits get on our nerves. Getting along can be a huge effort.

I'm not talking about uncapped toothpaste or underwear left on the floor. The issues at stake are more serious and run much deeper.

Relationships take work. This work can come in the form of fighting, talking, taking time for each other, and sex—yes, sex can be work! At some point, every relationship has to see these issues through.

During one of my highly discontented single years, I witnessed a bad first year of marriage for my friends Isabel and Thomas. They had known each other for several years before their wedding and had lived together, so it wasn't easy to predict that their first year would be as bad as it was. Their friends called them the Bickersons. Everyone witnessed their continual, unending spats, fights, and loud disagreements. They were unpleasant to be around; they were permanently at war. One morning they had a big fight about who was going to do the grocery shopping. Thomas came home from work and Isabel put a bowl of dried cornflakes on the floor for his "dinner." (I must admit, I still laugh at this fifteen years later.)

I never thought that kind of fighting would make a good marriage, but it did. They have two children, lost a third to a terrible accident during birth, and have weathered illness, family feuds, and building a house, their customized menu of both typical and tragic circumstances that come with life. I think that in that first horrible year of marriage, they fought through so much karma, fear, and power, their bond became almost indestructible. Now they are happy in a way that isn't staged or obvious, but in their easy sharing of family responsibilities, freedom, encouragement, and love, it's clear. They get along well, neither is afraid to be vulnerable, and both respect those times when not getting along is just a passing phase.

Each marriage is as individual as a snowflake, so it's impossible to say just what troubles you might encounter in yours. I presume that you're thinking of the several hundred issues that get on your nerves, but not one of them is really the crux of the matter. Here's where karma, power, and fear wait for you. They can help you diagnose your relationship discontent.

Ongoing Grumbles

No marriage is without its problems. Two imperfect people aren't going to come together in one perfect union, although there's a part of every one of us that hopes it can happen.

Couple problems provide a rich basis for comedy and drama, for heartwarming inspirational stories and for tear-jerking no-win sadness. Chances are you live somewhere in the middle with the rest of us, where you laugh, cry, and feel good and bad about your partner within the gray zone of "acceptable."

Ralph and Alice Kramden of the classic TV show *The Honeymooners* are stereotypically "happily married." They constantly complain about each other, lose their tempers, and "outsmart" each other—but they get along. Add your little ones to the mix and you have an explosive cocktail of needs, demands, responsibilities, and time pressure. You think that's easy?

Your marriage—or long-term relationship—isn't there only for your pleasure: it's there for you to explore your ability to thrive in a partnership, to open yourself to intimacy, to give, to take, and to share life with someone else. That would be called karma. If your marriage is pleasurable, enjoy it; your karma is fine. But if you go through rough times or face tough issues you can't seem to work through, embrace it. Your couple discontent is yet another growth experience to improve your ability to love and live richly.

Couple Energy

Here's a diagram that might help you evaluate your couple discontent:

$$\text{You} \longrightarrow \quad (\text{WE}) \quad \longleftarrow \text{Other}$$

Let's define "You" as you and "Other" as your partner, and the "WE" as the energy of a couple in sync with each other. The WE is important because it's where power and fear are shared. It's also the place where your values and beliefs are shared. It's a stronghold of your spiritual energy, where you actually have an energetic "being" of WE—it's not physical, but it's there.

A healthy WE doesn't draw attention to itself. You're happy together but you can disagree if you need to. You appear in public as two individuals who happily volunteer to be together. You can joke around one minute and be irritated the next. A healthy WE lets you be yourself at all times. A great WE would even help you become a better you.

Your WE is in good condition when, under stress or pressure, you can find a place to reach some understanding. You hear people say things like "We're not drinkers" or "We believe in going to church" or "We don't eat red meat." This is presumably a healthy WE where one person can use the WE word with confidence.

Contrary to the healthy version, the WE is in lousy shape when you feel you don't know your mate at all or you hesitate to speak as a couple. "I'll have to ask him what he thinks of that" in reply to a question about trying a new brand of toothpaste is not a good sign of a healthy WE. That's a big control problem. "What do you mean you think a gambling vacation is good family fun?" That's an issue of values. In an unhealthy WE, you won't use the word *we* so often. You might feel you're at each other's throat or that you aren't being heard or understood.

The WE is such a powerful energy, you can actually feel how it is affected when you're separated from your spouse or partner for a long time. If your WE is in good shape, you might feel weird and incomplete. It's also why breakups are so tough. You both have to dismantle and take back the energy that you put into the WE, like cleaning out a house you've lived in for a long time. It's filled with memories and intertwined experiences.

FUNDAMENTAL INSTRUCTIONS
FOR COUPLE DISCONTENT

- *Get back to the hill.*

  ๑ When you have couple problems, find your soft green hill and take time to reconnect. Just be together; hang out in a place that is familiar and acceptable to both of you, but not stressful or distracting. That means no TV, no kids running around, and no mud baths or hot tubs unless you both want to do it; if one of you is not at ease, it's not a soft green hill. Be careful of using alcohol or drugs here; you need clarity, not a hangover.

- *Feel what you feel.*

  ๑ Once you're hanging out, allow yourself to feel your love again. Find your heart connection, then speak. Share your doubts or concerns. When you speak from love (from the heart) and not from fear or anger, you will not only be heard, you'll have the best shot at resolving problems. The key to dissolving couple discontent is to work from the source of love, not anger.

- *Talk.*

  ๑ Declare your love for the other and confess your troubles. Weep if you have to. If you still don't feel heard or you don't see results—or if you feel your other isn't trying—try again and again until you're so worn down that you turn to couples therapy. And if that doesn't work, think about leaving.

- *Find the love or find the door.*

  ❧ You can take a test to find out if you even want to salvage the situation. Can you still feel love? Do you still feel loved? If you can't answer those questions easily, consider breaking up.

  In many situations you'll encounter together there is no easy answer, but if there is love on both sides, there is hope. Don't push. Both of you might just need a break, a time where other concerns of your life are allowed to take precedence for a defined time. It's a way of creating emotional space between you, a time-out that can give you both perspective and an opportunity to find new ways to approach the issues. You must define the time of your break, however, or you could end up farther apart. Give yourself two weeks, or wait until a big work project is over. When you reach an impasse, step back and take a break. The space you create between you won't be hostile, and you won't feel so pressed to solve it all at once.

The worst part of couple problems is when fear and power make you feel threatened and put you on the defensive (or offensive). You won't get anything done by tossing blame back and forth. In fact, that sort of poison can infect your WE and take even more time to heal.

Problems in couples need to be addressed by couples together. You can't go to couples therapy alone, now, can you? And I don't mean to suggest that you must go to couples therapy either. Both of you must see the problem. Both of you must want to solve it. Start to work on it by giving each other time to think or just to be. The space you give each other in tense times can be healing in itself.

Relationship Power Problems

Ideally, a relationship shifts back and forth in a pretty even flow of power. Maybe you're more powerful in one way but your partner has it all over you in another. That's fine. You don't have to measure up to the same level in every way.

Power problems are about control, who gets to choose where you go, what you do, who calls whom. No one person should call all of the shots. If you're the one doing it, you're acting out of fear and it's only going to turn on you. Try to control someone so he won't leave you and he'll leave. Being controlled by someone can feel relaxing at first (no choices to make or work to do), but eventually it becomes claustrophobic and stale. Power is to be shared—awkwardly, perhaps, but naturally. It's how we get to know each other. It's how we stumble and help each other up. Power-sharing is compassionate and trusting. Power-hoarding is controlling and distrustful. Power problems in a dating relationship are extreme and obvious pretty quickly. Don't stick around to watch it get worse.

My friend Julia once dated a wealthy businessman who was a known "catch." Julia is no wilting lily herself; she can stand up to almost anyone, but in this case, she gave the older, successful man the reins. He invited her to one of his country homes, a huge estate with a large staff. She was given her own room and bath, and the run of the house while he worked during the day. After a few days, Julia couldn't understand why no one had come to clean her bathroom. After all, the staff was all over the place, sweeping, dusting, and polishing. She kept her bathroom orderly but it needed to be cleaned. Even the trash was piling up in the wastebasket. Finally, she asked a maid to clean it but was refused. When her boyfriend returned home from work that evening, she asked him why. He confessed he had ordered the staff to stay away from her room so that he could see how well she kept it—if she cleaned it, if she straightened things. It was his little way of testing her to see if she was a good housekeeper and to see how she'd handle a problem. He had created a secret test, and to his surprise, he was the one who flunked. Julia was horrified and insulted by his underhandedness and she left without looking back.

Testing is a manipulative power play that undermines honesty. In testing someone, only one person is in on the truth—the tester. Whoever is being tested is just stumbling around in what he or she thinks is a real situation. It's not reality, it's a fishbowl, and it's simply unhealthy in any relationship.

INSTRUCTIONS FOR POWER PROBLEMS

Take your power back (or give his power back).
❧ Your choices here are simple. Call your date on any testing or power manipulations you suspect. If there's no response, it's time to break up. If you're the one controlling, be prepared to get dumped—because you will be.

Some power imbalances continue into marriage—which usually make for messy divorces. Don't do it. If you're continually finding yourself in power problems, see them for what they are.

Control is not love or concern. Control is not an element of a healthy relationship. If you are controlling or being controlled, what you have is not a relationship, but a grim imitation of one.

Cease the repetition; change what *you* do in these situations because you can't change anyone else.

Relationship Neglect

Another kind of couples conflict can crawl into your relationship and cause discontent before you even realize what's going on. I call it relationship neglect and it plagues couples with children and those who have been together for a long time.

Too busy to take time together? Guess what? It's time now.

My friend Cheta, now thirty-nine, has been married for twelve years. She once described the way she and her husband coped with their busy lives. They both work full-time, have two children, are personally renovating their ten-room Victorian home. They are also incredibly social and attend family functions all over the country. Listening to Cheta's schedule makes me dizzy.

When I asked her how she did it, she described how she saw her life.

"My husband and I are sitting on the floor, back-to-back with all our work and demands in front of us. We're both wildly busy, and

Romantic Love

we can lean back on each other when we need to be propped up. We share some work, the chores, etc., but once in a while we have to just stop juggling that stuff and really turn around and face each other. For a brief moment every so often we sit down together and do something fun. We leave our 'should do's' behind for a bit. It helps that my mom is a willing baby-sitter and that we have enough money to be able to get away for a weekend."

Their method is simple and it works. Take time for each other. Don't get lazy. Don't slouch off and go to bed early. If you don't take time for your WE, it won't be there when you need it.

If you know that you've run into those WE problems and you want to find your way back to each other, when you were both happy and satisfied, you can try some of these. They work only if both parties are interested in making the WE better. There's little you can do if your other won't play.

INSTRUCTIONS FOR DISSOLVING COUPLE DISCONTENT

❧ Your WE is like a live organism. We need four elements to sustain life: fire, earth, air, and water. You need all four of them to have a healthy WE, a healthy relationship. Let's take them one at a time.

1. Fire
❧ This element rules passion, energy, will, action, and heat. Fire gives you that oomph in seduction and the energy to care about your partner. Anger is fire-ruled, too. No fire, and you're just friends.

How to Diagnose Fire Issues
❧ Do you still want in on this couple thing?

Do you express anger? Passion? Do you laugh together? Does your energy match?

Instructions for Fire Issues
❧ Get moving. One or both of you need to take up jogging or kickboxing or something that literally shakes up your energy.

107

You'll feel more alive and alert, not to mention more active. Firing up your energy can fire up your libido as well and reactivate dormant passion and spirit.

2. Earth
🖎 Earth is grounding and it's vital for your health, physical being (and the myriad ailments that come with it), and sense of well-being. In your relationship, health can affect mood, emotions, and your ability to connect. It's got to be in good shape (I don't mean physically fit, although that couldn't hurt) for the WE to be in good shape. No earth, no noogie.

How to Diagnose Earth Issues
🖎 Do you have sex? (This is a must unless you have legitimate health reasons not to.)

Do you enjoy physical activities together—take walks, go bowling, go to fairs or museums, run a marathon?

Instructions for Earth Issues
🖎 Have sex immediately. I don't care if you have to force yourself. You need to connect with your other in this very basic way; otherwise you're still just friends. I heard a news report some time ago about a study that proved couples get along better if they have sex regularly. (You can choose the interval, but I suspect that once a year is too little.) You might also want to take stock of your physical health and get into shape. Being obese might be more socially acceptable than it used to be, but it's not healthy. See "Self-Esteem" if you need the push.

3. Air
🖎 Air is about communication and mind-sets. Are you intellectually engaged by your partner or are you bored yawnless? I don't mean you have to quote Shakespeare, but you need to have conversations—somewhere between "Where's my new sweater?" and witty repartee. Talk. Listen. Share opinions. Agree to disagree. No airing, no sharing.

How to Diagnose Air Issues
❧ Are you talking? Do you listen? Are you able to argue a point? Do you feel listened to? Can you agree to disagree?

Instructions for Air Issues
❧ You have to find a way to fix this. If you aren't being heard, if you're the one turning a deaf ear, you're going to Splitsville. That WE likes to be spoken to. You can learn about some tools for communication without too much effort. There are plenty of books in the self-help section of your library and bookstore (that you can read standing up), or you can invest in and read Dr. Phil McGraw's *Life Strategies.* If bibliotherapy doesn't work, get thee to professional help: you will benefit enormously from an objective take on your relationship.

4. Water
❧ In the realm of emotions, water is the flow that we need to taste our rich palate of experiences. Your water element has to be thawed to let you be in a relationship. All emotions live here: love, hate, sadness, fear, serenity—and anger likes to shift between water and fire so you can still feel angry when you're depressed. You can only account for your own emotions. You may be in the flow but your other might be on ice. Nothing you can do about that. Without water, you dry up.

How to Diagnose Water Issues
❧ Do you still feel love? Can you still feel love through anger or pain? Do you feel anything at all?

Instructions for Water Issues
❧ You must admit to yourself that you are either out of love with your other or depressed. Either of these answers is a tough road. To be safe, confess your fears to your other and check out the reaction. If your WE wants to stay put, you'll get instant feedback and probably a recommendation for therapy. If your other doesn't feel anything either, try going to the playground again and reignit-

ing the early feelings in your relationship. If you don't want to work on it or your other doesn't want to work on it, your WE isn't likely to be sustained.

It's About the Two of WE

You both have to be able and willing to stick it out. You have to have sex—it connects you in many ways and clears the way to feel your passion and love even more. You need to talk, to communicateso that you feel understood and your WE can be strong. You need to feel love—that's what it's all about.

Diagnosing the element that's out of whack can be helpful in deciding if you even want to pursue your relationship. Chances are, that element will show you how your relationship discontent is also about you personally. For instance, you don't have sex a lot because you feel bad about your body, and that's really a self-esteem issue that bleeds into your coupleness. But on the other hand, if you don't feel love and haven't for a while, it's time to think about moving on. You can't make yourself love someone, and you can't make him love you. It's hard to imagine falling out of love, but it happens.

Sometimes, just walking along the edge of leaving your coupleness can help you or your other see how valuable it is. It isn't easy to walk that far. You have to be willing to leave WE to get that true perspective. But just a glimpse of the aloneness that comes without the WE can rekindle all the golden feelings of love and hope that brought you together in the beginning. Seeing an end doesn't mean it's "the end."

There is always room for angelic intervention.

When Karma Is Played Out

In some cases, a karmic coupling will complete its mission—whether it was to bring children into the world or just to get two people together to work things out (on some level). You'll know when it's worked out because you'll know your WE is over. You don't necessarily feel any pain, you just know it's over because the decision is mutual, unbending, and inwardly peaceful (although it may be outwardly tumultuous).

It can be painful, however, to face that you've moved on, grown, or evolved in a way your other hasn't. I've seen this happen many times. One person is alive and thriving, growing from life's varied experiences, while the other shuts down, doesn't do any self-examination or isn't interested in working through life's challenges. This "shut down" option has to do with discontent that has settled into a depression. If you're the one who's shutting down, you're doing a good thing by reading this book—perhaps you'll take time to think about getting back into life again. However, if your other has shut down, there is not much you can do. You can't grow for someone else. You can't melt his discontent or even help him to see it. It's his own shadow to deal with, and no amount of prodding by you is going to shift it. You'll just frustrate yourself and your other.

If your partner is shut down, you have two options. The first is what you do when your WE was once strong—you wait it out. Go on with your life, see what you can do to gently show patience and support. Breathe patience into the situation so that you can allow your other to be shut down. Give yourself permission not to be your other's caretaker. Granted, it's a fine line between waiting patiently for the shut down to open up and allowing it to continue. Eventually, of course, you will want to put a time limit on your patience. Remember, you can change only you; you can't change another.

If, finally, you're fed up with the other, your love and your WE will be ready to split. You'll know when you get there. You can do nothing about someone else's choices. You can give your best, and you should, but you should also know when it's time to move on.

The Discontent of Breaking Up or Divorce

Typically, when you end a love relationship, you aren't experiencing discontent, you're experiencing loss. This isn't a passing feeling.

It's a painful separation of energies, a severing of that WE and a salvaging of the energy you put into it. You've been in a habit of being in a WE, and now you're not, and it's a big deal.

I'm not going to address breakups here because I believe that people need their own time and space to heal. Every breakup is different. Breaking-up and healing time relates back to how you deal with change—whether your mode is fixed, cardinal, or mutable. When you're ready to process the change fully, you will also be on your way back to contentment. Some people need to be alone and some need company. Each relationship you've had teaches you something (and it's more than "Yeah, I know, I learned he was a jerk"). A breakup is a painful growth opportunity because in the healing of your broken heart, you take on more wisdom and open to new levels of your creativity.

If you're the type to stay in a relationship until the WE has been dead so long it's dust (the fixed person, most often), you won't feel much angst at the initial separation. Don't be throwing any parties, though, because there will still be kickbacks and jolts of "Uh, we're not together anymore" that can hit out of nowhere. You might not cry, but you have to give yourself some time to heal, to get over anger, grief, betrayal—whatever negativity may come with the breakup.

Breakups have to heal on their own time. When you don't feel miserable anymore, go back to the beginning of this chapter and make sure you're not love infertile. Then go back to the playground and have some fun.

And you weary broken hearts, take note: don't get into another relationship too soon. You'll pull along that ghost of a WE from your last relationship, which will, in turn, erode any chance at building a new WE with someone else. Even years later, it will haunt you.

Family

ONCE your romantic love life is "settled" (and I use this term loosely), you are left to ponder the other relationships vying for your attention.

While romantic love is more mysterious and idealized, this other love can be just as frustrating and even harder to resolve. That's because it's usually about power—who has it and who wants it—without the allure, intimate magnetism, or romance.

Family ties are karmic. I've seen it proven time and again in astrological charts. Families have astrological themes in their signs and in subtle ties in the moon's nodes or planetary placements. Many connected karmic aspects can be found in a single family. Here's a living example. My mother is a Sagittarius with a Moon sign of Taurus. My father-in-law was born in a different year (and different country) and has a Sagittarius Sun, Moon in Taurus. My daughter is a Sagittarius with a Moon in Taurus. There are twelve signs of the zodiac to choose from, 132 possibilities, not to mention that my daughter was supposed to be a Capricorn but was born two weeks early. Somehow the universe managed to surround me with three people with the same astrological combination. I'm supposed to learn from them. I, on the other hand, was born under the sign of Gemini, the opposite sign of Sagittarius—the opposite of my mother, father-in-law, and daughter, and my Moon sign is Aries. Astrologically, I'm across the table from three close family members. The four of us participate in a Gemini/Sagittarius communications dynamic, which means we need to learn how to understand each other. Emotionally, the Taurus Moon is more patient and fixed than my Aries, impatient, combative Moon. We need to accept our differences, balance patience and willfulness, immobility and advancement.

Sometimes your family situation can seem like a club no one

invited you to join. Sometimes it might be the only place you're understood. However you feel, your family is the place where you learn about yourself, intimacy, communication and your values. So it's vital to get your discontents sorted out here.

Yet family discontents can be pretty much chronic. They appear and fade throughout your life. As you deal with them, you free yourself of those traps and pitfalls more quickly, and you can use that time for pleasure instead of complaining.

In general, dealing with this area of your life isn't a right-or-wrong proposition. It is a process in which you discover more about yourself and your capacity for love, patience, and acceptance. Instructions in this area might seem simplistic, even basic, because they go to the heart of who you really are and your ability to accept who your family is.

It will be hard to dissolve your family discontent if you think it's not about you, it's about them.

It's all about *you* and your ability to accept and love your family without condition.

The Club

You don't have to be a member of a close-knit clan to understand family problems. You don't even have to have big-deal issues with anyone in your family to understand the discontent that can arise from these relationships. It's fertile ground for alliances, strategies, secrets, manipulations, denial, power plays—you might think you've been playing in some soap opera, but it's your life, not the tube. Your family is the first group you belong to, the first club you ever join. You have a lifelong membership: they can't kick you out and you can't quit. You have to work with what you have.

It may seem unfair that some families have few problems and others, an endless supply. Don't bother comparison shopping. You can always find a "better" family or one "worse" off than yours—you're still stuck (or blessed) with what you were born with.

What can you do about this family of yours? You have to make sure that you know your boundaries—where you can say "not my responsibility" or "none of your concern." Most families have fuzzy areas where everyone has an opinion and thinks it counts. Can you imagine letting your family choose your career or your spouse? It happens in a subtle, shadowy way. Blurry boundaries are rampant in families.

Blurry Boundaries and How to Define Your Territory

A boundary is where you start and stop in your relationships. It's where the "None of your business" line is drawn, as well as the place where people feel free to enter your life in the capacity of "I want to help you" or "Your life affects all of us." When you're born, there are virtually no boundaries, but they shift as you grow up. Slowly, these invisible lines move outward—but parents rarely tell you that. No one ever issued you a card describing your position in your family:

"You are the designated son or daughter, and as such, you are to abide by the rules of this household. You are responsible only for yourself and your own conduct, and we are fully vested with your welfare, health, and education until you reach the age of eighteen, at which time you are an adult and we will renegotiate this contract."

You get used to whatever rules your household imposes and the boundaries that accompany them, and then you grow up. Even the healthiest people have boundary problems now and then. It's human nature and is reminiscent of the child we once were.

Your family has lots of unspoken boundaries; the more messed up things are, the more complicated the borders. For instance, in a family where a parent is an addict or alcoholic, you are exposed to these weird no-no's: "Never wake Dad up" or "Don't ask a question about . . . " Otherwise you'll violate the boundary that enables your family to keep Dad drinking (or gambling or whatever he's up to), and he might get angry, cause a scene, and lash out or leave. You learn to live by the rules of your club. You don't have to be in an alcoholic's family to encounter this phenomenon. You could be in the family that doesn't acknowledge issues about sex, money, or health. It doesn't matter. What is important is that every family has its own little web of "normal," and when you grow up, you'll realize that a "normal" family is a myth. Families are weird. What do you expect from this mysterious combination of personalities and souls that have no conscious say in how they got together?

FUNDAMENTAL FAMILY RE-BELIEF: IT'S A CLUB

❧ To begin dealing with your family discontent, consider this approach:

1. You have a role in the club.
2. You can change your role or resign.
3. You can attend club meetings at your own discretion.

The traditional family might be on its way out, but there's still a longing for it. Fathers and mothers are meant to be the bosses. Kids aren't supposed to call the shots. Kids aren't supposed to take care of anyone other than their pets or, when they grow up, themselves. Boundaries break when kids are forced to take on the roles of their parents. Kids do well with structure. They need someone to be in charge of club rules.

The Club Continues

Once you grow up, you get to start your own club. This is where it gets interesting. You don't just purge yourself of your childish methods when you grow up. You take them with you.

Ever wonder why you regress to being the "son" or the "daughter" or (in my case) the nasty teenager when you visit your parents? And if you are a parent, ever notice that you can't stop parenting your grown-up kid? The most brilliantly composed, sophisticated character can walk into a room full of family and regress into insecurity.

Family

Your family has a lot of control over you and it's not all good and it's not all necessary. That club is powerful.

Underneath the control of the family club is organic, real love, not conditional love as you might think.

Once you dissolve your club participation, you are released from your family's judgment and expectations. They can't *get to you* through manipulation, but they can influence you when they're acting from love.

Four Steps of Instructions to Dissolve Family Discontent

Step 1: Your Club and Its Members

If you're afflicted with familial discontent, the first thing you have to do is understand the roles of the club members and consciously resign from the organization. I don't mean that you have to quit your family, but you do have to quit your role in the family.

Everyone gets assigned some role—it happens unconsciously. This one is the Black Sheep; that one is the Smart One. He's the Golden Boy and she's the Pretty Face. You don't have to accept these roles and you don't have to play along with yours.

Just figure out the roles, figure out *your* role, then resign.

In my family I was the pleaser and the helper. I loved to clean and tidy up the house. I cleaned out my sisters' drawers with them, constructed useful bookshelves with my mother, and worried about everyone else. No one asked me to; I just assumed the role because I cocreated it with my family. It got me into trouble periodically because I would start helping when I wasn't invited to do so. I was a boundary invader.

INSTRUCTION #1: KNOW YOUR CLUB

❧ What are the roles in your family? Whatever they are, just stop cooperating with the group roles. Expect more from the Lazy

117

One and don't put up with the antics of the One Who Gets Away with Everything.

You don't have to convince everyone else to change. Don't get into a crusade to heal your family. That is not what this is about. Instead, look at it as an exercise in your own attitude. You don't have to get hot and bothered when the Lazy One doesn't do anything. Just say, "You're lazy," and leave it. The One Who Gets Away with Everything doesn't have to be accepted or endorsed by you. You can say, "When are you going to be accountable for your actions?" without feeling angry.

You have a choice. You might think that you don't. It doesn't matter how you've mentally grouped or labeled them (your mother the martyr, your father the controller, your sister the favorite, your brother the bum), your family members form a secret club in your psyche where their voices can resonate in your mind.

You don't have to let them have any say in your psyche or your life, and you can still have a great, close relationship with them. Really.

Step 2: Rules for Disengagement

The healing in your discontent is in your peacefulness with and disengagement from the club. You're still a member, but now you're the detached, even-tempered One Who Won't Be Drawn into Drama. Once you get angry and overinvolved, it's over. You're back in the club.

Here's the method you need to disengage.

I was inspired by a recent seminar at my daughter's preschool about the terrible two's. An accomplished child psychologist was discussing ways to deal with power plays that toddlers use. This is the kind of power play that you could laugh at, such as a child holding up a worm and dangling it over his mouth while watching for his mother's horrified reaction. My daughter liked to look straight at me while she dumped her food all over the floor. She laughed her head off.

The psychologist offered this advice to parents:

"When your toddler is trying to engage you in some sort of power play, don't look him in the eye. Just remove whatever the subject of the play is—food, a worm, a crayon, whatever it is—or remove the toddler from the situation, without acknowledging the toddler."

I puzzled at this information for a few minutes, then had a "Eureka!" moment. If you don't look a toddler in the eye, he doesn't get the satisfaction of your reaction, and the game is over before it's even been played.

INSTRUCTION #2: DO NOT ENGAGE

❧Toddler therapy is an apt method for dealing with your club's constant enticements to reenroll. Just saying no to your family doesn't work well, as I know from personal experience. What you need is a way to skillfully disengage from those constant offers to rejoin the club. Toddler therapy avoids insulting anyone and sidesteps power plays.

Adopt this insight into your family life. Don't look at your family (or the member of your club trying to engage you) in the eye. Don't play the game. Best of all, you can do this without making a big deal about it.

Here's an example. My friend Pammy has two sisters and a brother. The brother is the Golden Boy, Pammy is the Baby, and her sisters, Deedee and Sarah, are the Oldest (Accomplished) and Middle Child (Troubled) respectively. Sarah is the constant source of everyone's frustration because she's so good at the role of Middle Child and is hardest to get along with, or so it seems. No one likes to talk to her because there always seems to be friction or disagreements. As a result, Mom, Pammy, and Deedee usually talk about Sarah, what she's up to, how she's so different or how she doesn't cooperate. Pammy is tired of it. As the Baby, she always wants everyone to be happy and takes it upon herself to be the liaison among her mom, Deedee, her brother, and Sarah. Then she realized that she shouldn't have to be the One Who Talked to Sarah. She has other things to do. So she decided that she could deal with Sarah for herself but would not be the spy or conduit to the rest of the family. She tried the toddler strategy with her mother on the phone.

P: Hi, Mom. Did you have a good weekend?

MOM: Yes, it was great. Have you heard from Sarah?

P: Yeah, I talked to her on Friday.

MOM: How is she?

P: Great. What are your plans for this week? Are you around?

MOM: I don't have any plans. What else did Sarah say?

P: You know, I'm kind of busy. I don't know when I'll be able to get out to see you. Maybe we should put something on the calendar for next week. We could have lunch. (*Stay with your message.*)

MOM: That would be great. Will you ask Sarah?

P: You could ask her if you want. I have to go.

MOM: Why? Aren't you speaking to her?

P: Who?

MOM: Sarah. Should I call her about lunch or will you?

P: Give her a call. I'd love for her to come. Gotta go. Bye.

Pammy neatly volleyed the Sarah issue back over the net every time her mother served it up. In the past, Pammy would have called Sarah to set up lunch, called her mother to report on her conversation with Sarah, and be annoyed by it all. Now Pammy is using the toddler strategy and has gone as far as to tell her mother that she should speak to Sarah about Sarah. She has shared her plan with Deedee, who is giving it a shot, and the Golden Boy, but he's not interested. He doesn't have to make any shifts in his family place (yet) because he's not discontent. (He'll have his day.)

Step 3: Find the Shadow

In most groups, one person holds the dark side of the family: the shadow, as Jung called it. The shadow is the place where fears and mysteries settle. Cinderella held the shadow for her stepsisters by being the one who took on all the work and attracted nothing but anger and spite. Not all family shadow holders are Cinderellas, but they are probably misfits. It's an unconscious and, some argue, karmic role. Because everyone contributes fear to the family's shadow, the shadow holder can be a key to healing family discontent.

Shadow holders can be easy to spot. They might be fat, ill, angry, depressed, estranged—or they could be the middle child, like Sarah. They unconsciously hold the "dark side" of the family— anger, fear, anxiety—but it's all suppressed or repressed. The poor shadow holder becomes the dumping ground for everyone's anger, resentment, unfulfilled dreams, fears, and anything else that's unwanted. All the problems of the family are unconsciously assigned to this person. The shadow holders feel this role is natural. They usually don't try to fit in, they just do their best to put up with it or get out.

INSTRUCTION #3: FIND THE SHADOW HOLDER
(IF YOU HAVE ONE)

✎ Acknowledging the shadow in the family alleviates the burden for that person, but it doesn't heal the problem. Any person severely afflicted with a family's shadow needs real therapy and support. Family members each need to take back their own shadow—whatever fears or hatreds that were stuck on the shadow holder's shoulders. In Pammy's family, it would be like Deedee saying to Sarah, "I don't know why I don't seem to be able to communicate with you, but I'm sorry about it. I don't call you because I always seem to make you angry." That's just plain courteous. Before Deedee bothered to acknowledge her problems with Sarah, it was always Sarah's fault. Evolved people don't blame others for everything, and they certainly don't need to feel superior at someone else's expense.

Recognize that it's okay to agree to disagree. It takes the pressure off all concerned.

Step 4: Forgive and Move On

The last and final key to dealing with familial discontent rests in the all-important area of forgiveness.

Forgiveness is a big issue. It's pretty much the key to every kind of discontent you come across, but it's tough to get there.

The people in your family are always going to have the inside track in pushing your buttons. That's just the family way. You can minimize the impact of any negative influences by completely neutralizing them. That's through forgiveness.

You may not see it this way. You might be someone who comes from a difficult family background, with abuse, addiction, poverty. Or you could be more like my friend Pammy, with not terribly serious issues that are nonetheless chronic and problematic. No matter where you are in your familial discontent, there's room for forgiveness.

Forgiveness is tough but possible. It's hard to do it to someone's face, especially if she doesn't care to acknowledge her role in your discontent. And it's not worth it. I suggest meditating (just using a peaceful moment in your mind's eye) to forgive all the members of your family—and to let them forgive you. It's an easy meditation to perform but profound in its effect.

INSTRUCTION #4: FORGIVE

❧ You'll know when your familial discontent is lifted—and healed—when you can laugh again, at them, with them, among them. They are your club, and although you don't have to play on their field or participate in their games, you still have a lifelong membership.

Forgiveness Exercise

Define a time and space where you can be alone, undisturbed, and free to relax. No telephones, TV, computer, pager, cell phone, *nothing* by way of distraction. Find a comfortable position and close your eyes.

Breathe, unhurriedly and deeply, so that you feel your body relax more and more. With each breath, feel a calm spaciousness around you. Nothing feels tight, close, heavy, or anxious. Even thinking about the person who gets to you most is okay. You can handle it.

When you're ready, picture yourself in your mind's eye, walking along a road. Eventually, you will encounter one of your family members. As you approach the first one, slow your walk. Stop and see yourself standing composed. Speak your heart. You can say anything you like as long as it is something you can say you forgive.

"I forgive you for not encouraging my creativity and for not being there when I needed you. I forgive you for loving my brother more than me. I forgive you for not giving me college tuition. . . ."

Take your time. Run through whatever it is you want to say. When you're done, give this person a hug and say, "I forgive you," one more time. You don't have to say, "I love you," if you don't want to. This is only about forgiveness, not love. Take your time as you go through your family members. You can do them on different days or at different times if you like. It's more important for you to be ready to forgive them and mean it than it is to go through them all in one go.

Family Is for Life

Despite this forgiveness strategy, understand that your family discontent will come back. It follows you, looking for another way to infiltrate your life. No matter how hard you try to defuse it, you can be sure it will return in one form or another. Working on it makes it easier to deal with. Practicing the forgiveness exercise has its most profound influence the first time you do it, but it can always be "finessed" if you need to do it again.

And someday you might find yourself getting peeved like a first-grader and thinking, "For crying out loud, here I am again." But I beg to differ: You're not there at all. Once you have identified discontent and the tools that can heal it, you won't ever feel so powerless again. You'll have to practice catching yourself when the family pushes you into a corner, but soon you'll be able to finesse a dodge here and there. It's good to practice.

Laugh as much as you can. The humor in these little at-home dramas is really good. Once you see the humor in your mother's sticking her nose into everyone's business or your brother's delight in his chronic unemployment, you won't feel it so acutely. Don't look them in the eye, enjoy a little chuckle, and get on to the good part of your life.

Special Circumstances

Innumerable events or influences, such as physical or mental illness, addiction, estrangement, disaster—and many more hard-hitting, unforeseeable curve balls—can take your family from dysfunction to disintegration. If your family suffers a blow to its core group, such as the death of a loved one, or the departure or separation looking back, you will have to reorganize the club and sort out a whole new understanding of what you are. It's not simple. It takes time. Affected core members sometimes no longer want to participate in the family, especially if bitterness takes over.

Family

You can't make them; all you can do is adjust to the circumstances as best you can and get on with your life.

The traditional American family is now a minority. You might enjoy *Father Knows Best* reruns, but you won't find many living that life in reality. Families are no longer only a mother-father-and-children proposition. They are creative conglomerates of loyalty, devotion, love, dedication, sacrifice, and negotiation. Families are complicated. If you try to measure your family experience against a stereotype that is all but extinct, you will be sorely discontented. Don't fall into the trap of thinking that your family is the only weird and horrible club. There are many. There are also many that are cool, that buck the tradition of mother at home, father at work, impish kids at school. And they are happy families, too.

Find your family in other ways; be creative. Exercise choice and free will. Families are all about support, connection, and love. You're probably already a member of a club like that. While you can't choose your parents or your siblings, you can choose your friends. In many ways, they become your most important source of love and support as your life goes on. These are the people who believe in you and come to your aid without the club's rules.

Friends

UNLIKE family, you can choose your friends. You'd think you'd choose people who were just friends and not hard work, eh? Karma—more karma.

This isn't to say you can't have perfect friends who pick you up when you're down, be with you, talk with you, and share with you. They do exist. Some friends aren't hard work at all. Some are.

My friend Kristin recently met me for lunch. She's a new friend. Even though she's ten years younger than I am, we get along well. We laugh at the same things and have conversations that are easy but feel real. She told me about a party she had attended, one given by a "high-maintenance" friend of hers, and how she was tired and hadn't wanted to go but did because that's what being a friend is all about.

When I asked her what *high-maintenance* meant, she just shrugged. "You have to dress up, be very social, be flirtatious. It's very hard to describe. I just know what she's like and so I make sure I don't let her down."

That sounds like trouble to me. In friendships where you are either sublimating yourself to fit in or in friendships where you are clearly only there for one reason (because you're fun, the right age, the right business), you're heading for trouble if you think this friendship has roots. It doesn't.

I think that transient friendships can be decent and good. Like expectant mothers who bond in their Lamaze classes, you can have something powerful in common and offer strong and real support to each other, only to grow out of it and move into a different orbit. There's nothing wrong with that, as long as you appreciate it for what it is.

It is useful to think of your friends like the planets circling around you, some closer, some farther, some large and some tiny.

They shift and move about and aren't always within view, but they are there.

I think back over the friendships I've had over the years and realize how some of the strongest, most influential friendships have run their course, and how some low-key, always-in-the-background people have stuck around like Super Glue. If you take time to look back at your friendships, you'll see what I mean. Some people are meant to be in your life for a long time, and some people are there to light your way only for one part of your life. All of your friendships are valuable and worth understanding.

FUNDAMENTAL INSTRUCTIONS FOR FRIENDSHIP DISCONTENT: COMPASSIONATE DISENGAGEMENT

❧ You need only learn one basic principle for dissolving discontent in relationships with friends and working relationships. It sounds easy, but it is anything but.

I have come to understand that the troubled waters of friendship discontent can be handled with some understanding and some distance. I call this compassionate disengagement.

You have to acknowledge the difficulty, the situation, the feelings, the source of the issues at hand, but you have to stop trying to control the outcome or to solve the problem. Allow the situation to be what it is without taking sides.

Someone might need help or demand help from you, and you won't be able to give it, such as a friend asking for money "to survive" when you're only just able to take care of yourself. What do you do? If you can't handle his requests for money (let's say he asks you time after time and you sometimes give, sometimes don't), you're going to get fed up. You give what you can and even more than you should, but he doesn't see that. What he sees is someone who earns a salary; he thinks you have money all the time. This might make you angry. Your friend then becomes a source of discontent in your life because you feel guilty for not helping more or for not being able to help more, and angry at being asked to help so much.

If you evoke the principle of compassionate disengagement, you will be able to acknowledge his hardship:

"I feel terrible about your circumstances. I know this is a hard time for you."

And then address your disengagement:

"I have given you more than I can. I have my own priorities and commitments. You might think that they are not as important as yours are, but I have to do what I think is right. I cannot give you any more financial support, but I won't walk away from you."

For you to take care of yourself and your family, this is a necessary step. Once you start to compromise, perhaps offering some money but less of it, or allowing just one more loan, you're back into discontent. Stay with what you need to do for yourself and your family. It can hurt in the short run but will leave you with less guilt and anger in the long run.

You have to be at peace with that decision. You might feel some emotional kickback or some discomfort by sounding so final, but as you live with it and allow yourself to move on, your discontent will dissipate. Of course, you'll have to expect your friend's response. This can range from temperamental to petulant. Once he's expressed his feelings, let him get on with his life. You don't need to be his punching bag or to listen to his distress any more than you truly want to. Cutting him loose will give him more time to fix himself, and listening to his whining or complaints is a poor use of your time and his. Put yourself and your obligations first, be clear with your friend, and know that you are being responsible and compassionate.

Being able to look someone in the eye without fear or anger, without guilt or the need for approval, is essential to compassionate disengagement.

Those are only the basics for battles in friendship problems. Carry on for the finer points.

Friends Who Rank

One episode of *I Love Lucy* beautifully illustrates the discontent of friendship. Lucy and Ethel are appearing in some show for the benefit of their women's club. While readying for the performance, they accidentally buy the same dress to wear. The dress is lovely, with several layers of flowing, chiffon sashes, a flower, and several other decorative details. Neither will give up wearing the dress for her part in the show. As they stand before the audience glaring at each other and singing Cole Porter's "Friendship" through gritted teeth, they casually tear each other's gown apart, one delicious detail at a time. Of course, they were close friends (on TV) who apologized to each other right away. That is certainly not always the case in real life.

Friendship discontent varies in potency and meaning; you're not in the same club (like a family) and you don't have to be connected your whole lives. You'd think that friends would be easier to deal with. For the most part they are, but that's for real friendship, the kind that really goes through thick and thin.

There are so many different kinds of friends. There are work friends, sports friends, and school friends, to name some common-ground friendships. To me, relationships fall into four lists: Grade A, B, C, and D. Those people on the C and D Lists are most often contributors to your ongoing discontent, but in the rare instances those on the A or B Lists make trouble, it's usually major.

A List = People you know you'll always know and who are there for you when you need them. You can be away from them for years and still catch up in one sitting. These friendships are usually formed early in life (before age thirty) and last throughout.

The friends in your life who are completely cool with who you are and what you're doing are not going to register high on your discontent scale. This is your A list. They will understand your shortfalls and mistakes; they will support you during your difficulties and will celebrate your good fortune. You will do the same for them with a real, open heart. They aren't perfect, but they're unlikely to cause you discontent. They can get on your nerves at times, they can disagree with you or be angry with you, but forgiveness is pretty easy to muster on both sides. Think Lucy and Ethel.

B List = Common-interest friends, geographic friends, time-of-life friends. These are the people you grow close to for a finite time because of a common interest, a common neighborhood or lifestyle, or a common experience such as being parents of third-grade soccer players, for example.

The B List can be slightly trickier if you don't have a clear idea of the limits of the friendship. These friends can appear to be heading for the A List, but then—whoops!—you realize that you need to be careful about what you reveal or that there's a limit to how much you have in common. Sometimes it's just a matter of how long you've known each other. Friendships take time to cook, and the earlier in your life that you meet people, the likelier they are to be on your A List.

This isn't to say that people you come across later in life won't be close friends, but you're most likely to encounter B people. They can be great friends, but they aren't necessarily those you turn to in times of trouble.

My friend Billie uses a single question to define her A List: "Would I let them be my one phone call if I got put in jail?" If the answer's no, they're not in line for Best Friend Status.

By contrast, if B List people were dates, you'd enjoy the playground together but there would be no lifelong chemistry. No big deal. You only run into trouble when you expect too much from them or vice versa. They are probably nice people but not for your A List. They might not post bail for you.

Earlier, I mentioned my friend Kristin who was lightly complaining about her "high-maintenance" girlfriend. That's a B List friendship. Kristin feels obliged to show up and "be" a certain way even if she doesn't feel like it. A regular, good friend might be momentarily frustrated if she hadn't come to her party, but would have gotten over it quickly.

* * *

C List = Fleeting, "situational" friends, or transactional friends. This includes people you see casually, people you do business with, those who just come and go over a cup of coffee.

It's the C List that gets interesting. These "friends" are really acquaintances. They are in your life for a reason, and those who irritate you are there as a lesson. These friends might spur your discontent, but you can't shake them. They show up as a chronic annoyance (gum on your shoe), and you must deal with them but you don't want to know them anymore. Carlos Castaneda called some of the people on your C List "petty tyrants." They irk you or get to you in some way, but because we live in a civilized society, you have to put up with it. A coworker who is slyly competitive with you is a C List friend. She might deny it to your face but compete just the same. That feeds your discontent.

What I call "transactional" friends are also C List and are likely to seep into your discontent waters. These friends expect something from you. They aren't really friends, more like acquaintances or people who populate roles in your life that have power or influence over you. A C List friend can be the person who cuts your expense checks (be nice to her or you won't get your money) or your chiropractor who wants to be your friend (you want to risk a broken neck?) or someone even closer, where the transaction is harder to define. If you've ever been friends with a social climber, you'll understand this. You're her best friend until she doesn't need you anymore. A transactional friend wants something from you—respect, a favor, support, influence—and gives you something in return. It's not friendship, though. It's a friendly business relationship, whatever the "business" is about.

I attract a lot of C List friends because I'm friendly and curious. I like to know more about people than I learn in just a passing transaction. You can have a lot of healthy C List friendships, but of course you get some tough ones, too.

I make my own trouble with C Listers when I stick my nose in their business. I like to read tarot cards and look at charts—it's part of my curiosity and natural desire to give advice (which should be obvious to you by now). I like to do readings when it's my idea, but I get grumpy when I feel that I'm expected to. I'm not a party trick you can use when you feel like it. I always know when I'm in a transactional friendship when I'm expected to show up with my cards. I'm there to perform a service, even if I'm considered a friend. I usually take it in stride. I try not to make dates with expectant C List people if I'm not in the mood to give.

Your transactional friendships may be few or plenty—but you probably have a few. Just be aware that they aren't really built on solid ground. The only way to convert them to sturdy, real friends is to dissolve the transaction. Be warned, this can dissolve the friendship, too.

D List = Enemies. The people you know who drive you crazy or torment you in some way. They have a talent for establishing discontent.

It's a harsh word: *enemy*. You don't have to feel hatred or loathing for someone to be an enemy. In this context, an enemy is someone who inevitably causes you pain by some action or nonaction. They snub, they whisper, they don't stand up for you or else they imply that you aren't "okay" in some way. Your real friends—all of the A, B, and C Listers—will not listen to this nasty D Lister. But the damage is done. You will want to stay away from this person.

The Powers of Friendship

Ideally, friendships don't have a lot of power plays. A friend supports you and believes in you but isn't trying to keep you from going somewhere or using you to get somewhere. You can lean on a friend in times of need, and you'll give him or her your shoulder to dampen when a good cry is in order. Here are some questions to ask yourself about friends who are bugging you:

> *Do you support each other?*
> *Do you value the same things?*
> *Do you share a sense of humor?*
> *Do you tell them the truth even if it's difficult?*

If you answered yes to these questions, you're probably in a solid friendship. If you're discontented, ask yourself why. Perhaps that friend is shifting directions, leaving you behind. Or maybe your self-esteem isn't permitting you to be honest and to reveal your true self to the person you want to be friends with.

Friendships teach powerful lessons, mostly from the part where you don't get along. I'm going out on a limb here to say that, in my experience, friendship is a bigger issue with women than with men, but it's powerful for both sexes.

Women are friendship-dependent and like to talk, share, and compare with other women. Men aren't quite as gossipy and chatty but still need a number of male friends to be there in the background, ready to hang around, compare investment strategies, watch football, play basketball—whatever it is that they do. I don't profess to define or understand the motives or desires of all friendships, but I do know that both men and women can be bogged down by friendship discontent.

Trouble Among the Ranks

There are some pretty predictable causes of friendship discontent:

> *Competition/jealousy*
> *Triangles/power plays*
> *Unresolved anger*
> *Change of values or life direction*

Jealousy

Friends who secretly (even unconsciously) don't celebrate your successes aren't A List material. This isn't to say that you won't occasionally feel a little envious once in a while when someone attains a goal you've always wanted. But if you find yourself envious or covetous of someone who is your friend (or enjoying a feeling of superiority yourself), go straight to the section on self-esteem and don't look back.

INSTRUCTIONS FOR JEALOUSY

◈ If you are beginning to have problems with someone you're close to and can admit to jealousy or lording it over them, you're unhappy with yourself. It's best not to aggravate the situation while you're feeling tender; lay off contact for a while. Deal with your own feelings first and put your friendship on hold. Once you feel more at ease in your own skin, you'll be able to restore the friendship. Your regenerated spirit will then be able to celebrate a friend's happiness (or empathize with her lack) instead of widening the gulf between you.

Triangles

If you are in a triangle friendship, welcome to the land of power plays. It's not easy. I was in a triangle friendship for years, a karmic triangle of women. One woman remains an A List friend and the other, a B Lister I mistook for A List, is no longer a friend at all. That's classic triangle material. In a malevolent undercurrent of rage, jealousy, accusations, and misunderstandings, that friendship got nuked. My A Lister friend in that triangle stayed friends with us separately, so what was three is now a more comfortable and natural two and two.

In numerology the number three is an unbalanced number (as are all odd numbers) because there's no symmetry. With two, you can be one-on-one. With four, you can be two-on-two. But three is slightly clumsy. It takes constant focus to make a friendship of three work in the long run. It's possible, of course, but you have to be open and clear when you're angry or tense, because things can quickly shift to two against one, and that's dangerous. Working together, balancing three, is difficult. You can spot threesomes everywhere once you get the hang of it. There's the Boss, the

Worker, and the Assistant Worker on the totem pole. At work there's a real hierarchy. After work, you can socialize as if there's no hierarchy, but you're leading a double life. The totem pole is still following you around, and these people are never more than C or sometimes B List friends because your friendship is constantly put into a pecking order. Work is what binds you, connects you, and the Boss gets the last word. That's not to say you can't make friends at work, but you won't know how real or deep the friendship is until you're not working together any longer.

INSTRUCTIONS FOR TRIANGLES
AND TRANSACTIONAL RELATIONSHIPS

✣ Reduce the rank. If you're in anything that resembles a triangle or a transactional relationship, bear in mind that this relationship can go no farther than the B List and should not be considered an important, long-term friendship. If the triangle dissolves or the transaction disappears, the rank can rise.

Unresolved Anger

Perhaps the most sensitive and hardest friendship problem to resolve is anger. If a friend of yours harbors anger—at you or anything else in life—that friend is going to become a problem. The "Anger" section of these Instructions will help you if you're the one who is angry. The hard part of friendship is when you're not the one who harbors a grudge. You can't make someone come clean with you, even if you see that there is a problem. You can't make your friend talk to you.

Sometimes life heaps discontent on one person's life and he just can't handle it all. Without working on the problems, that poor soul is going to suffer from anger, bitterness, and/or a victim mentality. "Why doesn't anything ever work out?" "What else can happen?" Don't ask.

Friends

INSTRUCTIONS FOR YOUR FRIEND'S
UNEXPRESSED ANGER

❧If you have a friend who is going through a hard time and refuses to help himself, you have two choices.

First, you can try to help. You can gently suggest solutions, reflect on the issues, advise, support, or distract as much as you dare.

Then, you bail.

If your discontented, angry friend isn't interested in dealing with his problems, why should you be? You won't like this person anymore, you won't have anything to say (because you'll never say the right thing), and you won't have much in common because you're someone who likes to *deal with things.*

Get some distance. You don't have to be friends with someone who doesn't have enough energy or self-respect to take steps to get better. Sometimes people only get going when they get left alone. You don't have to be cruel about it. Just say your piece ("I want to be a good friend to you, but you won't let me"), and let your friend know that you're there if anything changes. Then take a break. You deserve it.

The Value of Values

Friendships also veer from the path because of a change in values. It's something you experience more as you get older, when your friends marry and begin to have children. My childhood friends stay home and raise families. I work. We keep in touch by e-mail and the occasional reunion, but there's no judgment about our differences. Our values were respected from the beginning of our high school friendship.

In another incident, though, I was startled by the abrupt departure of a college friend. We had been roommates briefly before she left New York City for another job. She got engaged to a nice guy a few years later and came to stay with me to catch up. We had a great time. While telling me about her husband-to-be, she talked about how much they had in common and how material things meant a lot to them and how making money was really important. While I have nothing against money, at that time I was leaving the advertising world to write about self-empowerment and delve into metaphysics. We were veering off in two different directions. To tell the truth, I was horrified by this old friend who was so driven by the need for money. So many other things in life and in the world at large seemed more important to me.

I know now that she has her large house and stacks of dough. At least she got what she wanted. But I don't know much more about her situation because we're not friends anymore. We didn't have enough in common to sustain us.

INSTRUCTIONS FOR A SHIFT IN VALUES

❧ If you sense a change in values, reduce your reliance on this friendship. This friendship will fall to C List if the shift in values is permanent.

Intolerance

The greatest threat to all friendships is intolerance. You don't have to contort yourself to get along with anyone, but you do have to be honest, open, and tolerant even when you're not in agreement. That's A List friendship. Even in B and C Lists, your tolerance level is important, up to a point. If your soccer pal is a little loud and rough around the edges, that's fine because it's all on the soccer field. Move into more personal ground and you might feel uncomfortable, the icy edges of discontent piling up. Your country-club manners might not match his pub-grub mentality. Are you intolerant? Perhaps, but you now have a boundary to your friendship (keep it on the field) and an insight into your own behavior. Laugh at your own "man-about-town" manners, enjoy that you can be at home in a down-and-dirty situation, and you're home free. No problems on that friendship front. But lasting sniggering or put-downs about your soccer friend's lack of finesse or judging his character based on his behavior is totally not cool. Talking about a friend behind her back isn't going to solve your discontent, either. It's intolerant, unfriendly, and shallow.

INSTRUCTIONS FOR INTOLERANCE

❧ When a friend is getting under your skin, assess your tolerance. If you can't handle it, you're not friends anymore. Don't mask your feelings. Distance yourself until you can be a true friend again.

GENERAL INSTRUCTIONS
FOR FRIENDSHIP DISCONTENT: BUBBLECIZE

❧ When you're feeling out of sorts with someone for whatever reason, try this exercise. It takes the pressure off and lets you get on with life.

Find a comfortable position and close your eyes.

Inhale and exhale, relaxing your body.

Picture yourself and the friend who is bothering you. See yourself sitting together with some space between you. You're not close and you're not far from each other.

Notice that you are each engulfed by a big bubble. You can easily breathe within this bubble. It's pleasant and spacious. The bubble contains just you but doesn't suffocate you.

With each breath you take, your exhalation increases the size of the bubble and the space between you and your friend. You're both still sitting down, relaxed. Each exhalation creates more relaxation, more distance.

Keep breathing until the bubble is as big as you want it and your friend is still within your sight but is far enough away that you don't notice what he or she is doing.

When you feel comfortable with that distance, open your eyes and return to reality.

What you've done in this exercise is to create breezier and easier psychic space in your friendship. Even if you see this person every day, you should feel less oppressed by your discontent and possibly even more tolerant. It's hard to keep balance and distance when your problem is in your face every day, so repeat this exercise as often as you need to.

Betrayal

With different types of friends, there are different levels of betrayal. Treachery by a C List person might not devastate you like the disloyalty of an A List friend. Still, betrayal is tough to bear in any situation.

I always think back to adolescence, those days in junior high and high school when friends become more important than anyone else. The wounds of mean-spirited kids can live with you for a lifetime. Preteen and teenage friendships can last a lifetime, too, but more important, the bad ones can set the stage for deep-rooted discontent.

Once you grow up, you realize that you don't have to be liked by everyone, that those "cool kids" in high school don't usually lead very interesting lives (my theory is that a lack of early discontent makes them lazy). As an adult, you make your own friends and choose whom you want to be close to. Then, one day when you're not looking, someone pulls an adolescent punch on you and you're plunged back into insecurity.

To my eye, men do this to each other by subtle competition and psychological games. Women do it by gossip or social sabotage. I can't comprehend why anyone takes pleasure in betrayal, but it still happens. When my daughter was born, I made friends with a few first-time mothers at the park near our home. We made dates to meet once a week. After a month or two, I found out that one of these new "friends" had been bad-mouthing me and my daughter around our neighborhood, and that as a consequence, we were excluded from certain play dates and socializing. I would never have believed anyone would be so ridiculous and malicious, but I was confronted with the naked truth by my baby-sitter and another mother who took pity on me. I felt humiliated and hurt, which I can live with, but since this involved my baby daughter, I rose like a lioness and confronted this woman with a phone call. As you would expect, she was a coward and denied it with curious dispassion and disinterest. It took me quite a while to heal from that; it hit me right in an old adolescent wound, kids whispering about parties I wasn't invited to. I used the bubblecize exercise above to give me some psychic space between me and the other mothers and the following Instructions for expelling enemies to give me peace.

INSTRUCTIONS FOR EXPELLING ENEMIES

❧ In one or two windows that face out from your home or office (or both), place mirrors reflecting *outward*. This is to reflect any evil energy and send mal-intent back onto the person who sends it. While this may seem like a symbolic gesture, it gives you ample peace of mind because you have taken action and, furthermore, it has strong psychic effects. Typically, evildoers get their own toxicity right between the eyes.

I heard that Mean Mommy was eventually short on friends because she pulled her stunt one too many times. Not that I care (much).

Big-Time Betrayal

In some ways, being betrayed by a close friend is on a par with getting dumped by a grand love. Like a broken heart, betrayal by a trusted friend can be devastating. You need to recover, to work through the slam to your heart and your life, and to heal. This isn't discontent; this is pain. There's probably a karmic element here, possibly a power play, almost always a fear motivator, but when you're enduring a brutal blow from someone you loved and counted on, you won't be able to see that. Just breathe through the rough times and, if you need to, get someone to help you sort through the rubble. Then, when you're better, go to the exercise for forgiveness (in the section "Family") and see how far you get. Healing is all about forgiveness, but it takes time.

Isolation and Loneliness

At times in everyone's life, discontent settles into a feeling of loneliness. Since discontent is so purely personal and internal, it makes sense to feel a little "different" or even isolated from people around you. Even if you're married or among lots of friends, or even if you have a big, supportive family, you can still feel alone.

The alone time that discontent brings you is usually a profound healing experience, although often painful, and usually not quick to lift. You have to sit with yourself and feel that pain or hurt or whatever it is that your discontent brings you. No one else, no matter how much he or she loves you, can feel it for you.

It passes.

I know that sometimes it feels as if it won't, like a stubborn broken heart or the ending of some association that seemed imperative to your whole being.

Isolation and loneliness are common healing side effects that provide a time of reorganization for your emotional energy. It's a cleansing, a rest for your heart and probably your karma. I assert that every pang of hurt you feel dissolves some karmic obligation, so it effectively makes you lighter when it's over.

Being alone creates stillness within you. It's a great time for forgiveness meditations and for allowing what you're feeling to rise to the surface. You can discover old interests or longings buried beneath the surface of your consciousness. Remember, though, that isolation and loneliness can lead to inertia. It's hard to get motivated about life when your cheering section is empty and you have no one to play with. You have only yourself to spur you on and get you out in the world. That's hard for anyone to do. But that's what these Instructions are all about: get up and get out.

INSTRUCTIONS FOR LONELY SPELLS: GET OUT

- *Be active.*

  ✒ Do a walk or ride a bicycle to raise money for charity. Volunteer your time to an organization that can use you. Join your company's baseball team. Run in a corporate challenge. Simply take a walk around your neighborhood.

  Being out and about has two positive effects. First, you lose that inertia. Being with your personal energy in an activity, particularly outdoors, makes you feel part of life again. Second, your participation in anything—even just walking around—brings you back to the "land of the living."

- *Connect in other ways.*

  ✒ Volunteer. Being with people in the spirit of giving of yourself is an effective way to put loneliness on hold and even make new friends. The internal rewards from doing volunteer work will help offset feeling isolated.

  Try the Internet in moderation. I don't think it's a bad idea to find your own cyber-community, but it won't completely solve your isolation issues. Staying home because you have no one to hang out with is not a good answer. Surfing the Internet because it's easier to make friends there is not good, either. Yes, it takes you to a place where you can find like-minded people and where you can find some solace or entertainment. But if you want to flow in the stream of life outside your window— in the street, on the sidewalk, at a park—get off your butt and get some fresh air.

Work Relationships

They're not quite friends, they're not quite acquaintances, they're not quite family but sometimes they feel like it. You sure see them more than your own family.

They're your coworkers.

Almost all of us grow up and get a job. Even if it's a volunteer job, you find yourself working with other people. You don't necessarily get to pick them, and you sure don't know if you like them right away.

To simplify matters, let's define work as anything that isn't family, friends, or love relationships. It can be your religious organization, your career, or the PTA. It is a group of people who come together for a common purpose but don't necessarily do so to be with each other.

Everyone thinks they go to work for a reason—to make money, to accomplish something. The teacher is there to teach, the teller is there to cash checks, the doctor is there to heal. Sure, that makes sense. But there's a whole lot more to work.

It's all about karma, power, and fear—again. Interacting with people in situations that may generate stress or fear is a great karmic teacher. I've learned more about myself and I've encountered more karma at work than in any other place in my life.

Look at the people you've encountered at work. Some of them might as well have been born on another planet. At times they seem like textbook examples of psychiatric cases, and occasionally they're deeply disturbed con artists. Of course you're going to find normal people and mentors and even warm, long-term friendships, but that's not where discontent likes to live.

Work is not just work. Work has a steady flow of current karmic relationships and personal testing grounds for you to work out your issues.

Got problems with sharing? Welcome to Teamwork 101.

Issues with freedom? Here's a job with a time clock.

Want to be the boss? Here's a nice subordinate position.

Deserve credit for your work? Need to prove yourself to abozo? Stay late just to look good? Play politics because it's what you have to do? Ever have to pay dues when you already deserved to be promoted?

You name the game and it's here: power plays, being seen, heard, respected, accepted, getting along with those above and below you. Work always has a hierarchy, no matter how many roundtables you have. Someone is the boss and a lot of people are not.

I've been in dozens of work discontent scenarios myself, and they all boil down to some combination of power, fear, and karma.

Ultimately, though, the Instructions are simple.

If work is getting you down, look at the power/karma/fear issues beneath the surface and you'll be able to diagnose and treat the situation.

Power

Typically, if you're discontented with the power in your workplace, you feel you don't have enough of it. In a hierarchy, you have to accept that you don't get equal voice to those above you. Work is not a democracy. Power is about having influence, and all you can do is voice your opinion (or e-mail it) to someone who has more influence to add to yours.

INSTRUCTIONS FOR POWER ISSUES AT WORK: LET GO

If you cannot sway anyone or you have no opportunity to voice your opinion, you have two options.

1. Disengage your emotional attachment to the issues.

That means you have to say and mean, "I don't care."

2. Leave.

Work is not a place to be used and abused. If you have strong, principled disagreements with those in power, do not stick around. Work should not be a test of endurance. Rest assured, your life will not be free of discontent if you are pouring your power into your work and no one cares.

Karma

You're going to run into a parade of karmic relationships all along the work front because power and hierarchy are part of work. It's truly one of karma's favorite playgrounds. Some good karma is there, of course, which is when you're happy and feel compensated and appreciated—and there's no discontent. It's in that tough, hardworking karma where work discontent likes to breed.

Instructions for Your Discontent

Difficult working relationships are created by karma. If you can't get along with someone no matter how hard you try, you're looking at karma.

Discontent caused by karmic relationships is either going to heal and dissolve or sit there like a boil on your back, irritating you without reprieve.

To heal a difficult work relationship, you need to disengage from your "need-demand" issue, whatever makes getting along so necessary. Ask yourself, "What do I need from this person?" or "What do I demand from this person?"

If you need approval or acceptance for a non-work-related reason (such as you want to be "one of the boys" or asked out to lunch by a certain group of colleagues) and you're not getting it, stop wanting it. I know this is easier said than done. If you think that you must have this respect, acceptance, or whatever it is you're not getting, reevaluate your motive for needing it. You're not going to get what you want, so change what you want.

INSTRUCTIONS FOR KARMIC ISSUES AT WORK:
RELEASE THE NEED

When you stop caring, the dynamic will be gone and the energy will shift.
❧Chances are, the other person will shift into a more agreeable state when you stop participating in a need/demand situation. Don't be surprised if that person tries more than once to engage you in the same need/demand again—you might be goaded once or twice to slip into it. But once you stick to your resolve and avoid the "I want to be your friend" or "I demand you do things this way" (or whatever your need/demand source was), you will be discontent-free within days. Stop caring, stop despairing.

If you cannot, for the life of you, put a stop to this dynamic, don't stop trying. Leaving won't help. You will only run into another source to bounce your need/demand karma off of, and you'll have the same situation with a new player. Karma will rear its head wherever you go so you can try, try again.

Friends

Karmic situations that involve your emotional engagement are not going to go away with turning your back. It's time to face them, work on them, diagnose and treat them. That's what disengages the karma and the discontent.

Fear

Your fear in any work situation has to do in part with survival (I need this job! How will I put food on the table? Pay my mortgage?), which, within reason, is absolutely normal. You want to work because you need to survive.

If your fear surfaces in other areas, too, such as the emotional areas of the need for acceptance, belonging, esteem, and even self-actualization, you need to deal with more than just work discontent. These fears are there for you to face and they will follow you wherever you work.

INSTRUCTIONS FOR FEAR AT WORK: FIND THE SOURCE

❧ Fear is there for you to explore. If it's not a survival fear, what are you afraid of? Ask yourself the source of your fear. Is it the need for approval? A fear of abandonment? Is it based on a need to be accepted or validated?

Here we enter the murky waters. It's where you might want to attribute the cause of your discontent to someone else, but, in reality, it's all about you. You must recognize that the people or events around you only stimulate the problem that already exists within you.

Fear in any relationship—in romantic love, with family, friends, or coworkers—can be a symptom of discontent that is more internal, that of your self-esteem. If you fear losing someone's friendship or approval because you need her to make you feel worthy or valid, you're basking in discontent that has nothing to do with her and everything to do with you.

Your Instructions are in the next chapter.

Your Own Instructions

Part III

You

You've already explored a great many of your personal issues in the areas of prosperity and love. Almost every matter of discontent is linked to your self-worth, but the layers of your life make it hard to see that.

Now that we've stripped away the two most common causes of discontent, we can confront those more sensitive areas that require your honesty, integrity, and courage.

It's hard to face yourself. It's hard to be honest about what you really fear and what you really doubt. Forget hiding behind "If I only had enough money" or "If I only had a decent relationship, I'd be fine." It's time to look in the mirror and like it.

The following chapters deal with discontent you might not have considered before. Read them. You will no doubt find yourself. You will nod along. And you will be more at ease if you follow these Instructions.

Self-Esteem

WHAT do you think of yourself? Do you hold yourself in high regard or in bare contempt? Are you consistently supportive of yourself or does it depend on the circumstances? Self-esteem is at the core of many of our discontents. When you act from good self-esteem, that is, when you feel positive about yourself, you'll probably act with integrity. When you act from low self-esteem, you might make mistakes or poor choices, which leads to more low self-esteem. We are reluctant to say to ourselves, "Good job! Fabulous! You're a star!" and all too eager to say, "You little putz, can't you do anything right?" But we shouldn't.

I can't tell you how many times I've wormed away from the question "Do you love yourself?"

From the wrong person, that question can sound cloying and smug. Regardless of who asks, it's hard to answer.

Loving yourself is simply not something that you consciously think about.

RE-BELIEF #1 FOR GOOD SELF-ESTEEM

๛Self-love, self-esteem, is an evolving appreciation of who you are and demands a strong degree of acceptance. Allow yourself to be the imperfect person that you are—no shame, no fear about it.

You are lovable in spite of what you might perceive are your weaknesses. Look around you. The people who are happy aren't exactly physically perfect, nor are they supersmart or even supernice. They know who they are and they are willing to be loved for that. And while they may not love being rejected, they don't sweat it.

Laugh If You Love Yourself

I believe that this kind of self-love is facilitated by a sense of humor, but it is not absolutely dependent on it. If you have to rely on just self-acceptance, apply a large dose of forgiveness instead of laughter and you'll have the same outcome.

While feeling bad about yourself can be the greatest fuel to getting what you want out of life, it can also be your worst enemy. Discontent over self-esteem is a huge learning opportunity—and a continuing one. Once you recognize your low-self-esteem behavior, you'll see it again and again in yourself, and in others. Identifying low-self-esteem behavior in yourself makes it less powerful. Recognizing it in others makes it easier to forgive.

Once you see your pattern and forgive yourself for it, you'll see the humor. It's really amazing how karma puts you in the same patterns again and again. You'll start reacting differently, less seriously, less strictly, and that leaves room for pleasure, contentment, and even laughter.

I've been insecure with the way I look since adolescence. I had a "fat" period back then, and that fourteen-year-old girl still likes to make an appearance in my self-esteem. Even today, I can feel perfectly happy with the way I look, and as soon as I walk out onto the street, I can have my self-esteem shot to hell. I live in a neighborhood with lots of modeling agencies (that's New York City for you), and it's not uncommon to see a model walking four steps in front of me. She's six feet tall, weighs about two pounds, and looks ready for a magazine cover even in her sweats. Boom, my fourteen-year-old fat ego steps in and I feel about two feet tall and spherical. What four seconds ago was my healthy, thriving body is now a lumpy, lumbering, ungainly mess. No one did that to me; I did it to myself. Twenty years ago I would be in a bad mood from it. Today I shake off the temptation to turn around and hide under my bed. I laugh at my reaction. Just don't ask me to try on bathing suits right away.

What Is High Self-Esteem?

Being in good self-esteem doesn't sound so hard when you think about it. It's about feeling capable, responsible, powerful, open, and emotionally available. It's a balance of your mind, heart, creativity, and emotions. If they are all open and flowing, you're probably in good self-esteem.

The theory, however, is easier than the practice. You have to be real, respect who and what you are *authentically*, and apply self-care, self-respect, and self-worth accordingly.

When I was in high school, a particularly challenging time for most of us to deal with our self-esteem issues, I really wanted to conform and fit in. I tried to emulate the majority, wearing clothes that didn't suit me, summoning enthusiasm for sports I didn't like, drinking beer I didn't want, building the homecoming float I had no interest in. I constantly studied popular kids to make sure I was measuring up on the latest slang and jokes. To this day, a part of me wishes to be a conformist. I confessed this to my husband during our courtship, and he laughed so much he fell off his chair. I guess he could tell I was pretty awful at it. By then I had done a lot of work on myself and had started living more authentically, which, in my case, was pretty nonconformist in leaving a successful career in advertising to try my hand at writing and astrology.

Over the years, I've grown accustomed to being a little outside of the mainstream. It's relaxing. It's a lot easier than trying to fit my square peg into a round hole.

RE-BELIEF #2 FOR GOOD SELF-ESTEEM

You're a square peg and everyone else is, too.
꙳ Your differences, not your similarities, make you who you are. Embrace those eccentricities, honor your whims and opinions. They are the most interesting parts of you.

You don't have to live outside the mainstream to realize that you belong only to yourself, and, as much as you permit, to your family and your chosen friends. You don't have to meet anyone else's criteria to be valuable. You don't have to be accepted by everyone, either.

Belonging

It's always nice to feel you have a group of friends or colleagues who are there for you. But if your self-esteem is low, you can take this too far. When bonds you have with other people or groups take on a deeper meaning and make you feel better about yourself, you're in for self-esteem discontent. Your group of friends is now used as a protected club or a symbol of who you are or what you believe. Your belonging starts to rely on too much outside yourself. The group opinion starts to be your own. Where's your free will, your choice? The group's preferences, activities, and even beliefs might be wrong for you. What can at first feel like a cozy, warm crowd can become suffocating or isolating. If the group's power becomes more important than your individual preferences, you are definitely in trouble.

Yet many of us want to be accepted by certain people in order to confirm that we have standing among them. This happens at work, in professional organizations, volunteer groups, politics—in every walk of life. It's a human desire to belong and to be valued. You have a legitimate claim to this fulfillment. But what if you don't get what you want? What if the crowd doesn't want you? Or if they kick you out? What if the crowd's mentality starts to conflict with your own? You have to move on with your self-esteem intact. That can be difficult, but not impossible. What if you don't get into that professional society you want? What if you're not elected to the board? What if you're not "cool"?

The Cool Police

The notion takes root early, as early as second grade. Children sort themselves out into best friends, groups, and cliques, but their definition of "cool" changes from generation to generation. It could be the jocks or the techies, the debaters or the artists. There's always some group that seems more powerful, more alluring than others, and the kids who aren't a part of it feel left out.

It doesn't improve much as you get older. Office politics often define an "in" crowd. It's human nature to cluster and bond, to find friends with common goals or shared opinions, but sometimes those clusters are exclusive, snobby, and cold.

The need to be cool as an adult isn't evolved behavior. Those people who cling to cool are feeding a hierarchy akin to the counterprosperity notion of "there's not enough to go around."

Compare and Despair

Good comparisons and judgments are no better than the bad; in fact, comparing yourself to others isn't useful at all. For all I know, that gorgeous model walking ahead of me had an eating disorder (that's low self-esteem) or is in a failing love relationship. My longing for physical perfection and my unwillingness to accept my own form is a loudmouthed demon (now with a muzzle) who lives in my self-esteem. Comparisons and tacit competition always leave someone diminished.

Bolstering yourself by rating someone else "not as good" isn't going to give you strong self-esteem. It just feeds the notion that you're competing with the world for your own self-worth.

Cool people can exist only if they make their club exclusive. They have to set up an "in" and an "out" or there aren't any boundaries and then no one is cool.

It takes a great deal of energy to be cool, to continue to feed the cool boundaries. Whole industries have sprung up to support cool: jeans, sneakers, nightclubs, private lines to restaurants, publicists, magazines, movies, art, and music. The minute something catches on and all of us are "in" on it, it's not cool anymore.

Here's your choice. You can participate and spend a lot of time keeping up and, by consequence, hand over your free will and let someone else tell you how to dress, what to listen to, what to think is good, or whom to praise or criticize. Or you can just do what you like. I vote for the latter, of course. It's so much easier and tons more fun.

Cooperating fully with the cool police is a sign of weak self-esteem. Not that you can't like the cool stuff or have genuine connections to things that are cool, but you should do so only because it's authentic. You have to really like it.

I constantly run up against cool living in New York City. In my twenties I tried a whole lot of cool groups to see if I would like them. I went to art openings in cool galleries, nightclubs of the moment, sporty jaunts such as football games, tennis matches, and charity hunts, and lectures at various museums. I went to some things just to see what it was like, not because I was interested. I wanted to get to know the world and develop my personal tastes. I learned what gave me genuine pleasure and let go of what I didn't like. It's normal to try the cool stuff when you're young.

As you get older, you become cool by really being yourself. Cool isn't being different to be different, it's being who you are as a result of your life choices. It isn't keeping up with the styles, it's establishing your own. The adults who cling to the notion of cool often end up looking anything but. Looking cool and acting cool is best left to the kids who dictate and change its definition.

If you're under twenty-one or even twenty-five, you may well suffer at the hands of groups and cliques, cool people or "out" folks. If you're older, get over yourself. It's not attractive or productive to care about being cool—and certainly not a sign of someone with good self-esteem.

INSTRUCTIONS FOR GETTING OVER COOLNESS

- *Examine the cool person in the cold light of day.*
  ‰ Let's take today's great lions of cool: celebrities. They have cavities and a lot of cosmetic dental work. Some don't have great educations. They can be riddled with drug use, unsuccessful relationships, and secrets they hope you won't ever know. They have tabloids digging up their garbage and report-

ing on it. Are you sure you think this is cool? They have no privacy and, as a result, insulate themselves with people they have to pay to be loyal and discreet. They have more transactional relationships than you and I do, and even their families and friends don't always have a place in their world. It's a lonely way of life because being cool, even if it's thrust upon you, distances you from being normal and average.

- *Remember what they're famous for.*
  ❧There are a lot of nonacting celebrities, people famous for their crimes or their deal-making, their designs or their ability to hang on in a reality TV show. Remember what they are famous for. Simply being famous is not carte blanche for being a life expert. Don't lose your sense of self and power by assuming these people know more than you do.

- *Ask yourself if they know what they're talking about.*
  ❧Do you want to take financial advice from someone who gained credibility in a completely different area? Do you want a model to give advice to new mothers? Do you want an actor to suggest what kind of herbaceous border you should choose for your home or whom you should vote for? I think not. Celebrate people for what they have accomplished and respect that, just because they're famous, they aren't knowledgeable about everything.

- *Look to others for examples, not goals, and ask for guidance, not formulas.*
  ❧If you wish you were someone else, you aren't even near content. Remember, you are all you have. Nothing will change who you are, and you won't ever be happy until you get to know and like yourself. You can be successful, popular, admired, or revered if you find and nurture your own power. To yearn for someone else's life is just denying yourself your own path to happiness. It's fine to admire others, but they don't hold the answer to your perfect life. Be assured that they have their own karma, power, and fear to deal with.

Remember the girls in junior high school who used to travel in clumps? They'd dress alike, develop similar speech patterns, even laugh the same way? That's typical teen behavior where adolescents cling to shared habits and outfits to feel as if they belong. Even though it's superficial, it suits that age group. As an adult, that kind of behavior only shows how little you think of yourself. Your taste, style, and preferences can be guided by what you see, but it's your choice you have to exercise. Your choice is all the power you have.

COOL RE-BELIEF

❧ Being happy with yourself is cool, no matter how much of a geek you think you might seem to others. The true geeks are people who lead their lives looking for validation through others' approval.

Rejection/Dejection

With healthy self-esteem, you sustain disappointment and realize that rejection isn't the final word on your value as a human being.

With low self-esteem, rejection deals you a blow to your core and it's harder to recover.

How you handle rejection is a strong indication of the strength of your self-esteem. The world consists of so many different opinions and beliefs, you're going to run into a few you don't care for, and there will be those who don't care for you.

The more emotional the relationship, the more painful the rejection. If a stranger's rude behavior makes you feel bad, you're going to feel even worse when your boyfriend doesn't remember your birthday. In low self-esteem, you wonder why that person you didn't know was so mean to you and if you could have done anything about it—and you think it's your fault that your boyfriend is an idiot. You take it all on yourself. In good self-esteem, you ignore the stranger and you tell your boyfriend exactly what you think of him.

Discontent plays a big role here. Where your self-esteem sinks, there is a little work to do in your life. When your self-esteem is in good shape, you can usually rebound from the hard knocks and pit-falls that come your way before you get to discontent.

The Power of Vulnerability

Oddly, the formula for being happy with yourself is found in fac-ing your vulnerability, not building your strength.

Most of us will make great efforts to avoid feeling vulnerable. When you're in any situation where you want things to go well or you want to make a good impression, you'll naturally do whatever you can to feel secure. Few people want to draw attention to their weaknesses, especially with strangers. Even fewer of us can handle being publicly singled out, wrongly or not, and staying calm. Lots of people can't even speak in public because they feel that's too big of a risk. They are not comfortable with their own vulnerability.

If you have read the Instructions on love, you won't find this too difficult to grasp. Being unafraid of yourself, of your life, of your choices, that's good self-esteem.

Releasing whatever keeps you from being who you are is within your power. You can do it. It's a matter of telling yourself the truth, accepting it, and laughing with it—laughing with yourself.

It's hard, after being brought up to distinguish between "right and wrong" and "good and bad" to find that almost everything is gray. There is no cut-and-dried answer to anything. Most of us are bundles of diverse and eclectic talents and traits that make us unique. When you feel insecure with your bundle, you might want to cover yourself up, hide what you're not comfortable with so that no one will see it. Here we have the beginnings of inau-thentic behavior.

I was always a good student, but in college I hated studying. Without a lot of effort I was a B+/A- student. Yet I wanted to be an A student and I was uncomfortable with my grades. I became a know-it-all as a result of my insecurity with myself. I tried to offer information to anyone who would take it (on any subject in which I could be the least bit convincing) just to prove to myself and to others that I was smart. I eventually learned that I *am* smart and that

I don't have to be a big mouth to prove it to me or anyone else. I also learned the power of one phrase, "I don't know." Admitting that is truly liberating—and smart.

For me, understanding that you don't have to have all the answers to be smart was a powerful insight. I stopped hammering at myself with that dreaded internal voice about not being smart enough.

I still have those moments of feeling inadequate, but now I try to find the humor in them. I accept that I'm not a great cook—so I order in. And that I may be good at math but I take no interest in it. That I love to learn languages, but I don't have a great attention span when it comes to grammar. And that I don't understand a lot of modern art but I enjoy the creative process.

Yahoo! I don't have to know it all. Fine. It's more relaxing just to be me. My discontent evaporated when I accepted my limitations. You only have to admit the weaknesses you're trying to cover, then wear them comfortably, like a well-fitting suit.

Beauty and Your Inner Beast

Part of self-esteem has to do with how you look, or, more accurately, how you perceive you look to others. Are you good-looking? Do you think you're good-looking? It matters as much as you let it.

We live in an appearance-obsessed culture, where the rules of beauty change every five minutes. You can get into a lot of self-esteem trouble if you try to keep up with fashion. You need to understand that standards for beauty are transitory; there isn't one person who fits all the criteria, all the time. The next time you see how beauty is defined, decide for yourself if you agree with the picture. This is the time it is right to judge beauty, and you don't have to like what the image makers are showing you. You create your own terms of beauty in your life, and that is all that matters.

Everyone wants to be attractive. Through the ages, both men and women have pursued treatments and adornments including makeup, jewelry, piercing, and tattoos to enhance appearance. Standards change. Whereas it was attractive to be heavy a few hundred years ago, being thin came in vogue after the industrial revolution. You can keep up with the trends or ignore the common beauty standard. It doesn't matter as long as you feel good about the way you look.

Discontent is going to rear its ugly head in your appearance self-esteem now and then. Men lose their hair. Women get cellulite. We all gain weight and lose our youthful looks. But what are you really losing?

The Value of Beauty

Beauty has its assets, certainly, but it also comes with a truckload of liabilities. Beauty opens doors, attracts attention, and gets you noticed. But beauty also pigeonholes people as vain, shallow, unapproachable, and even stupid.

People who are good-looking or beautiful can be deeply insecure because they may think that they are liked or loved for their looks. If beauty is an asset, other people want it. Men and women refer to good-looking dates as "arm candy." Do people want to be with them because of the way they look or because of who they are inside? Who wants to be just arm candy? What happens when the candy ages and gets stale?

We all want to be attractive, but at what price? It's not an easy answer because looks are a part of you, but not all of you; you can't separate your looks from your heart and soul. If you trade on your looks, you're going to get what you ask for—a relationship or job or situation based in part on your being good-looking. Do you want to get a job as an investment banker because you have a good face? If so, be my guest. I know that I'd rather be known for my ideas than for my big brown eyes.

I don't mean to say that you have to feel sorry for hunks and babes. But if you figure that your life would be easier if you were beautiful, you're wrong. You'd have a whole new set of insecurities and self-esteem issues to deal with. And you'd lose your looks anyway because you get older and that's just what happens. Aging will be revisited in the section "Time," but it's worth mentioning here that self-esteem issues might roar like wounded tigers as your looks fade and you get "old." The irony is, you'll look back on your youthful photographs and wonder why you ever doubted your appeal.

Reflection Objection

For those of you who look in the mirror and start critiquing your flaws: cut it out. There is no such thing as ugly. I know that severe disfigurement can cause great stress on appearance (and I believe this is out of the scope of these Instructions), but I know that no one is really ugly.

There once was a blind man who lived in a small village. He had no wife. In this village lived a woman without a husband. She was considered very ugly. The villagers set them up together. The blind man got to know her, fell in love with her, and married her. One day, a healer came to their village and offered to help the blind man see again. The villagers were all nervous that he would be angry when he realized they had married him off to such an ugly woman. But they didn't stop him and the blind man's eyes were healed. Instead of anger, he felt great happiness and he thanked the villagers for giving him the most beautiful woman in the town. He saw his wife with his heart, not his eyes, and his love was true and deep.

Self-Esteem

One person's "ugly" is another person's ideal. For every old sock, there's an old shoe. For every face, there is another one smiling back.

So forget that critical eye in your mirror and stop wishing your nose were straight or that your eyes were bigger. Forget perfection. It's expensive to attempt and impossible to maintain. Appreciate who you are, what you do have, how well you're aging now that you've released so much discontent in your life.

When Age Matters

Once in a while I find myself walking behind a cute young girl in tight jeans and sneakers, her blond ponytail swinging over her sweater set. I get a look at her face. Come on, lady, are you trying to scare me to death? Seventeen from the back and seventy from the front? Or a sixty-year-old man wearing the latest slacker/surfer duds with a shock of blue on what's left of his hair. There is something rewarding about growing up, people: you're supposed to gain better judgment and a little something we call taste.

As you age, low self-esteem can make you do all sorts of wacky stuff. You could try to feel young by keeping up with youthful fashions, or cling to what worked when you were young. What was beautiful to my teenage eye had a lot to do with Farrah Fawcett hair and heavy eye makeup. What is beautiful to teenagers now is completely beyond my understanding. It's the aesthetics of a new generation. Let them stay there.

What we consider to be beautiful evolves and you should, too. Your life is about developing the inside of you, not the outside. Make the most of what you've been given and look yourself in the eye (in the mirror) and search for the real beauty inside you, the kind that survives into your old age and doesn't require nipping, tucking, skin creams, hair grafts, or lack of personal style:

Strength
Integrity
Truth

Creativity
Humor

If those assets belong to you, your self-esteem is just fine. Go
ahead and color your hair, even get the little eye-lift if you want to.
Remember those steps won't improve your self-esteem, because
the way you feel about yourself is actually inside your skin. It's in
your heart and mind.

Inner Whispers

There's probably a voice in your head right now saying, "That's a
load of hooey." Oops—now it's saying, "But you don't really have
good self-esteem, do you?" And then it will say something like
"Yes, I do. No, I don't," and so on and so forth.

Everyone has a little voice in his head. It's saying all sorts of stuff,
some of it helpful, much of it useless. You can't help having that
voice. It's your thoughts, your wishes, your intuition, your mother,
father, and every teacher or leader you ever had. Some of them say,
"Good for you!" but oddly enough, some of the voices that shout
the loudest are negative: "You're never going to make it." "Who do
you think you are?" "Don't bother, you'll never get it."

You even get to make up your own voices: "You're so stupid."
"You're a weak pig for eating that cake." "You're never going to be
pretty."

A lot of dialogue is going on in there. It's a wonder we can con-
verse with anyone else with that racket.

Your inner voices have a dominant role in your self-esteem
issues. If your negative voices are overwhelming, you don't think
too highly of yourself.

How do you make them shut up?

Self-Esteem

INSTRUCTIONS FOR QUIETING
THOSE MEAN-SPIRITED VOICES

❧You can't get rid of that constant narrative, but you can give it a rest. Just a few moments spent in quiet-mind can be beneficial for many days ahead. These Instructions are simple and easy but they require that you set aside some time to *do* them. It's amazing how often those voices can whisper distractions to keep you from quieting them down.

- *Meditation.*

    ❧It's not a crunchy, health-food word. It's a practice of quietness and it's really easy if you take baby steps. There are two ways you can quiet those voices in meditation.

    Guided-tape meditations.

    ❧These are available at bookstores and even some libraries. Buy a tape, get a stereo, sit on your sofa, and listen up. By allowing someone's soothing voice to guide you through a few minutes of tranquillity, those inner voices get a rest. Your mindfulness, focus, creativity, richness of personality, and depth of character all get a chance to stretch their legs to walk around and find more energy. Meditation brings a lot of hidden inner assets to the surface. Once your inborn talents and sensibilities become clear to you, you are more powerful and more authentic. Everything in your life becomes clearer and your negative inner voices don't get as much airplay.

    White noise or breath meditations.

    ❧If you can't or don't want to use guided meditations, you can try using background white noise or nature sounds to lull you into a meditative state. This is more difficult, because you have to focus more on your own breathing and consciously quiet those intruding voices telling you "Remember to turn on the dishwasher!" or "I forgot to buy milk" or "This is really stupid!" I find it most effective to imagine that my inner voices are being herded into a soundproof balloon that floats away from my head and sits in the corner of the ceiling while I focus on my meditation. It may sound silly, but for me it works. You're the boss of your voices; they're not the boss of you.

There's Always Time

When I have no time to meditate, I do it when I wake up in the morning or when I'm going to sleep. I lie on my bed, focusing on my breathing, listening to my breath, releasing my thoughts, just allowing myself to be. This isn't optimal because I always fall asleep, but it's better than nothing. It's hard to find time or to justify the time to sit down for fifteen or twenty minutes to meditate a few times a week, but if you can do it, it will change your life. You'll like yourself better and you'll like your life better. It's a great dissolver of discontent.

Frauds

Many women and men have the strange, silent trait of feeling inadequate or fraudulent.

These people often ask themselves, "What if they find out I'm a fake?"

Even highly successful people are prone to question the legitimacy of their success. You might hear things like "What if I'm not really good at this and I've just been lucky?" "You're only as good as your last case." "There's always someone better coming up from behind."

This unforgiving, inflexible belief is a deep layer of fear. It breeds discontent and attracts the very behavior you want to avoid. Your fear can make you into a fake. Your fear can put you in a situation where the legitimacy of your success is questioned.

Fear is powerful and has an amazing way of manifesting itself.

You can't make fear go away, but you can soften it, open it up, allow room for other feelings.

If you are a secret self-doubter, have a conversation with yourself about your insecurities. Try to give some credit to those who believe in you; they aren't stupid. Don't obliterate real accomplishments because they don't fit your self-image of being a secret fraud. Your image is wrong.

Responsibility for accomplishment can be scarier than thinking you just got away with something. Accepting responsibility is the way to dissolve your discontent:

"I did this. I might not be able to do it again, but, golly—I did this. Hooray for me."

Most of your fears of being a fake are because you're afraid you won't be able to repeat your results and sustain success. I can solve that problem for you right now. People who take responsibility for success will tell you that they have already known failure. It's part of life. Most successful people know that failure is going to happen and that it's part of the game. It doesn't make your successes any less legitimate or you any less of a person.

Allow yourself to be vulnerable in your life and you won't be mowed down by failure. Allow yourself to be vulnerable and you will be able to embrace success and take it in as your own accomplishment, not just a fluke.

Good Deeds or Needy Deeds?

I have a classic "helper" mentality, where I will clean the entire house, take care of some annoying paperwork my husband can't seem to handle, make a few phone calls to secure reservations or make a doctor's appointment, whatever might be needed. I do it all voluntarily. These are good deeds, *nice* things. But they tire me out, since I've run around and tried to anticipate every possible detail that might affect my family's comfort. Then my husband comes home and does not notice any of the fabulous things I've done for him and our family. While he'll thank me if I tell him (which I don't: What's the point of asking for thanks?), he'll inevitably put his foot on one of the homemade land mines I've buried and blow us all up.

"Did you get a chance to pick up the photos?" he'll ask. Or "Hasn't anyone watered the plants?" Or "I wish you wouldn't turn on every light in the house."

It doesn't actually matter what he says. To my ears, it's always critical, another mark against me for what I didn't do as opposed to praise for my marvelous, superhuman achievements. I don't keep my reaction to myself.

"I just spent the whole day making your life easier and it's never enough, is it?" (You can fill in the next five minutes of my loud frustration.)

When I pause to catch my breath, my husband responds with his own discontent download. He's at work all day, dealing with slow computers, unhealthy cell samples, and other problems, and he has to ride the subway, which is horribly hot, dirty, delayed, etc. We are having a contest to see who has suffered more and neither of us wins.

I end up not only tired, but completely discontented. It's that nasty lesson:

No good deed goes unpunished.

If I had done all that work, those good deeds, without the hidden need for a pat on the head, I wouldn't have been so annoyed. I didn't use direct communication ("Hi, sweetie, I just spent the day doing all sorts of efficient things for us. I'm pooped"). I did a good deed with the silent demand for gratitude.

What do you do to get attention? Do you do things because they're nice when you really want to be noticed? Do you have hidden motives? The next time you want to extend a helping hand without a specific request, ask yourself whom you are doing it for. If you just want to be nice, is it because you just want him or her to be nice to you?

Low-self esteem can keep you busy, exhausted, and still unacknowledged.

The Weight of Discontent

I know this subject well.

Discontent, particularly with self-esteem, is a weighty issue and is very much about how we feel—light or heavy, lithe or docile. Moving energy is happy energy. Stilted energy is discontent.

Your weight can make you discontented, but it doesn't have to. If you are active, balanced in your life, and not endangering your health, you need not be discontented with your weight. If you walk out the door and feel fat because you think everyone else is so slim, or if you try on bathing suits (an unforgiving test) and hate your body, welcome to discontent.

Of course, feeling fat and unhappy is only the beginning. Go on a diet and you've taken the second step to discontent. After all, dieting can make you feel deprived. Several weight-reduction programs don't encourage deprivation and they can certainly work. But if you do fall off that diet, you're in stage-three weight discontent: you've given yourself something else to feel bad about. Dieting is difficult. You need more than just your discontent to make a diet work.

Before we plunge into weight Instructions, take a quick look at yourself. Be honest.

If you're not really fat or overweight, say so. You don't have to be overweight to feel fat, but you need a realistic assessment of yourself. If you just want to "lose a few," you can be just as crabby as someone who needs to lose one hundred pounds. You might feel fat because you don't get enough exercise or you eat heavy foods too often. Feeling fat doesn't mean you are fat.

Be truthful to yourself about what you really want. I wanted to stave off my forties by losing ten pounds. I lost eight pounds, but guess what? I'm still getting older. My fat self-esteem got tied up in my aging issues. Some people have fashion issues (fitting in the right clothes), romantic issues (finding the right spouse or keeping the one you have), or health issues—and health issues are always a good, sound reason to lose weight.

You can have any motivation you like, but if you have discontent somewhere else (like my aging issues), it won't go away with the pounds. Dealing effectively with your sluggish "fat energy," however, will free you up to do more with your life and get some other discontent out of your way

It doesn't matter how fat you are, if you have a fat energy, you're going to feel it and it will eat up your self-esteem.

INSTRUCTIONS FOR WEIGHT SELF-ESTEEM

❧ The solution to self-esteem lows due to fat is simple. You have to find your inner calm, your resolve.

A small, quiet, firm voice buried under those layers of fat energy says, "It's time to do something about this." This quiet voice takes over with determination, but not anticipation. It just says, "It's time."

Resolve puts aside all those little yelps and whines from negative voices saying "Just one cheeseburger won't hurt" or "You're always going to be heavy, why bother?" or "You'll never be what you want to be."

We all have resolve, that calm voice within, but we often don't listen to it because so many other things are in the way. Once you get a handle on this voice, it stays with you. It says, "No, we're not going to eat that because it's not the right thing to do," or "You got through an evening without a piece of chocolate. Awesome. Keep going. You're right on track." You don't even find a diet hard to follow.

Look deep within yourself to find your voice of resolve. It's not loud, angry, pushy, or seductive. It's just a quiet, firm, loving voice that says, "Here, we're going to fix this now."

This voice of resolve is not instructive. It doesn't tell you, "Go on a diet!" or "Get yourself to the gym." It says, "Come on, you can do it. You will do it," with a smile, not a bark.

You're unique, resourceful, and you know what you should do. You'd have to live under a rock not to be aware of unhealthy foods or the need for exercise. You probably know when enough food is enough. You don't have to be a genius to figure out what eating habits are going to make you feel better. Your resolve isn't a diet or a regimen, it's an internal power source that makes you able to dissolve your discontent.

Your resolve isn't always easy to find, however. It can appear out of nowhere, but it can be elusive when you look for it. One winter I hit on my resolve when I hated how tight my jeans had become. I didn't want to feel that bad about myself. I considered getting help from a diet center and then just hit on the weird internal button that said, "You can do it yourself." I ate healthy, low-fat salads at lunchtime, I had a small afternoon snack, and I stayed away from my chocolate supply. I took exercise classes and I enjoyed feeling lighter each day.

For some people, this resolve finds its voice when they see themselves in photographs. For others, it's discovering that life is shortened by unhealthy habits.

You can find your resolve by discovering the voice that says, "Oh, come on. You know you're going to get this done."

Once you find that voice, you are going to be successful. You can use whatever diet or coach you need to get there, but make no mistake, it's your resolve that will take you. Your resolve is the voice beneath all of that discontent. Let it be heard.

You Are No Judge

In any self-esteem issue, no one, including yourself, has the right to judge you. If you believe in God, you can designate that deity as a judge, but no person can do it. Your self-esteem isn't a criminal or civil offense that demands impartial consideration. It's a living part of you that needs attention—it's how you value yourself, not a proposition that is either right or wrong, good or bad. You can't define yourself with any single word and be accurate or fair.

You are not objective about yourself. You are not going to come up with a dispassionate appraisal of any part of you. That's why you have to believe in yourself, take your side in tricky situations, and accept yourself as a positive contribution to humanity.

Taking criticism and learning through being wrong is part of being human, but it's not meant to diminish your worth or your value. In fact, it's really there to stimulate discontent to help you evolve. Even if you think your best function here on earth is taking up space, you have to explore that function. No one is a total failure; no one is a real loser.

We are here to explore reality in whatever way it comes to us. If you don't respect that your life has meaning, no one else will either. And one life is no more important than another. You might want to argue that some world leader, inventor, warrior, or artist is going to live forever in the minds and hearts of all people, but that won't happen. Plenty of those types were around a few thousand years ago and most of us have never heard of them. Even if we have, it's not the pharaoh who lives in our memory, it's the pyramid.

Your self-esteem is at the crux of how you handle discontent. If you are a defender of your life and an explorer of experience, you will conquer your discontent naturally. If you don't give yourself enough support or if you don't respect yourself enough to address and work with your discontent, you will banish yourself into the limbo of depression. And that will truly be your loss—and ours.

Time

I DON'T have time for this. I have to get to work. I don't have time to get this house in order, do the shopping, sift through long-ignored paperwork. I don't have time to make dinner. Let's order in. Who has time to do anything these days? I sure don't.

I'm not alone. How many times a day do you complain about how there's just not enough time to get it all done? Live your life! Love, work, explore, build, enjoy—who has room for it all and still has time to do everything else? You don't, do you?

Time is a precious and rarely negotiated commodity. We take what we can get. We "make the most of it" when someone reminds us to.

Discontent comes when time seems too scarce or too long or too wasted, and it is not something you can ignore. If you do, you run out of it.

Let's step back and look at time objectively. It's not "your" time or "my" time—just time. Endless time.

Time Is Not a Clock

The subject of time can make you sick to your stomach. I'm not referring to those moments when you look at your watch and wonder how on earth you're going to be *on time.* I refer to the whole *concept* of time. You probably haven't given it much thought, but you should.

Think, for a moment, about how we mark time. Think about how the hours, minutes, and seconds are man-made measures. Back in the days of the dinosaurs, they didn't have clocks, watches, or sundials. The sun rose and set, the weather probably shifted as it does now through the seasons, but they didn't have "five o'clock" or "noon." They didn't have years or months either. That's just fine for dinosaurs, but did you know that back in early societies, people marked time by full moons (market days) and new moons (stay at home because it's dark out there). In winter months, when there was no market at all, they didn't even count time. They just waited until a certain full moon fell in the right constellation and it was time to go to market again.

You might be mildly amused by this information, but not impressed. That's all right. I want to get you started with the idea that time, our time, is just an artificial measure we impose on ourselves. No one is right. Lunar calendars get you to tomorrow just as easily as the Gregorian calendar we now use.

Time, in the greater sense, is endless. In the news, there's infrequent discussion about complicated theories of the beginning of the universe and how our universe is expanding and how our sun will one day die. But that's not the beginning or the end of time. You can't put your finger on when time started. Just because the universe might have begun with a big bang doesn't exclude that something might have existed before that bang; certainly time existed on some level. Even if you believe in creation theory, and that God created man, God might have been doing something else before He created this, right? You can't say for sure. The Bible starts only at the beginning of this world. God might previously have been employed.

There could be time warps or wrinkles or blips in time; who can prove there aren't? Time is just not something you can explain or take lightly under any circumstances. Time requires your respect and attention, appreciation and acceptance. Time flows endlessly; it doesn't stop when your watch battery runs out.

I certainly have no desire to convert you to my love of contemplating time and its ultimate, infinite, impossible meaning. I only ask you to realize that the world has gotten along well without marking time before and that your world can use a little of that, too. I hope you can be nudged into a more flexible frame of mind. If you're willing to see time as more elastic and not so linear, you won't feel so fenced in by its pressures.

Perception

Time has a great deal to do with perception. Ten minutes in a doc-tor's waiting room can feel like a month and a half. A friend of mine suggested that we do away with naming the months of October, November, and December and just have one month called Autumn, because time flies by so quickly then. On the other side of that coin, we could use two or three more months just to break up January, February, and March. As you get older, time passes by so fast you can barely pace it. An eight-year-old might think a ninth birthday is a thousand years away, while you can ask people over forty how fast the year goes and they'll just shake their head with amazement. Your sense of time accelerates as you age.

Accept that your perception of time has a lot to do with your relationship to it. Is it your enemy? Are you racing the clock? Is time passing so slowly you can see paint dry? If you bring an attitude to your dealings with time, you will have it reflected back to you. Surely you want to be friends with time, don't you?

Pacing Time

T. S. Eliot wrote about measuring life in coffee spoons. I find that mine takes its pace from holidays and estimated tax payments, holidays being the markers of "Oh my gosh, I have to do *that* again? What should I cook/wear/buy, etc.?" Seeing turkey deco-rations going up around Halloween steals three full weeks from my calendar. Estimated tax dates, like rent or mortgage checks, are pinpricks in your consciousness that bring up discontents around prosperity as well as time passing.

When I worked in advertising, I lived a full three months ahead of most people. In publishing, editors and marketers live about a year ahead. If it's spring outside your window, sales forces across the country are being introduced to the goods you'll be buying at Christmas. Commercials are being produced, print ads being shot, scripts being evaluated for products that aren't yet born. If you add

177

up all the people who work in these industries or others like them, you'll realize that a large part of our population is anticipating events that won't happen for some time. Even at the parents' association at my daughter's school, planning and executing a fundraiser for November starts in May.

This may seem harmless to you, but if you are continually tracking time and thinking about what you're going to do in the future, you are neglecting your present. If I'm writing a book to be published in a year's time, going to meetings about something that will happen in six months, and thinking about Fourth of July barbecues in May, who's taking care of what's going on now? We all have enough "future" going on that we don't have as much "present" as we can use—and need.

Losing time to planning is a die-hard habit. We've been programmed to think about what we need to do ahead of time because otherwise it won't get done. Baloney, I say. Everyone is running around worrying about overprogrammed children when we, the adults, are suffering from being programmed to live ahead of time.

Revising Time

When was the last time you let a whole weekend go by without plans? Or took a spontaneous vacation? Or didn't talk about what to have for dinner until the moment you got hungry for it? Not everyone is guilty of this behavior, but if I've hit a nerve with you, take heart. You might want to rethink time. First of all, let's dispense with what you know.

> There's no time like the present.
> Today is the first day of the rest of your life.
> All you have is today.
> Time waits for no man.

Fine. Every single sentence is true. But can you live it? Sometimes it takes a sudden death to get it, or a scary medical diagnosis, or a disturbing news story or a movie with a powerful message. We all have that nerve of mortality buried somewhere inside; the question is, how often do we dig it up and remind ourselves what it feels like?

You can consciously understand that your life is happening right now (and not yet under the Christmas tree next year) but still succumb to that busy-ness that takes you out of it. Unlike money, love, and self-esteem, where events or opportunities can rock your boat into the waters of discontent, your relationship to time is all about you, baby. *You are fully accountable.* Yikes! How does that make you feel? Frankly, I find it a little scary.

TIME RE-BELIEF

❧ Time is your own natural resource. Only you can decide what to do with your time—no blaming anyone else.

As you read this, take a breath and notice the seconds count away on the clock. They just keep going. Time is like that.

I hear my friends complain about how they have no time. Once you have children, it seems your time is their time, and if they don't need your time, someone (or something) else does. That pretty much sums it up. Or does it? You must learn to say no to others when you need time to yourself. You're no good to them if you're cranky or underenergized.

If you're so accountable for how you deal with time, why don't you have any? Surely if you had so much control, you wouldn't put yourself in such compromised, impossible situations. You choose to have a family, to work (if you have that choice), to see your friends. Where does all the time go?

It's still there, but it's not responsible time. It's not that dreaded term *quality time.* A lot of the time you're doing what you have to do to get to the time you really want: a date with your loved one, a hot bath, a good book, a jog. I hear myself say it all the time: "I'll just get all these horrid errands done and then I'll have time to . . ." I might as well be an eighties throwback who says, "I'll just make my first million and then I'll have time for my family." That attitude is no more ridiculous than mine. If I'm going to do errands, I'm going to make the most of them and I'm going to enjoy them; if I don't, I won't do them.

Here is your choice. Do you have to take your dog to the groomer on your way to pick up the dry cleaning (it's right next door), then drop off baked goods at the school before your tennis lesson (and before that sprinkle of water you call a shower) so you can get into the car to start carting your kids around all day? Or do you want to be content?

You can fill in your life with perfection and efficiency and be miserable. Most of you know that.

The Art of the Slacker

Slacking has its place. One day I'm going to start an association of slackers so that this art form (well-performed by a certain younger generation) can be celebrated in the ranks of well-meaning adults who strive for the good life and end up with a mood disorder.

Cut out the "must do's," "should do's," "want to do's," and do what you can without forgetting your own time. This is not new information, but you're still not doing it, are you?

Until my slacker support group is off the ground, I suggest that you ask yourself the kind of questions you might use to remember your prosperity. When confronted by a day of obligations that you don't like, ask:

Is it a life-or-death need?

Will anyone in my family suffer if I don't do it?

Will I treat people better (including my family) if I'm not always in such a hurry?

Am I doing something because I'm telling myself "It's easy" when it's really not?

Is this a "good deed" that I will be punished for?

Is there something I'd rather do with my time?

Chances are, nothing is really life-or-death. You have to do some things that aren't fun, like mammograms and dentist appointments, but they give you better quality of time in the future if you take care of them. But if you're looking to buy wrapping paper or stationery, or shuffling between social engagements you don't care about, cancel them. Call in favors if you need time off from the car pool. Or let your kids miss something; they're programmed, too. Start teaching them about rest, free time, and knowing when to take a break.

I'm not suggesting that you ditch all responsibilities and obligations. But if you don't have a little time to do nothing once in a while, you're going to ooze discontent and someone you love is going to suffer for it. And you're accountable. Just say no when you need a breather. It's your life.

Boredom

And now for the other side of the coin. It's a rare moment when your old pal boredom catches up with you. He's sure not racking up frequent guest nights at our house, but once in a while a certain "blah" feeling descends over me and I know he's back and I know it's not really boredom, but discontent.

My four-year-old daughter has learned to use the concept of boredom to get her own way (not that it works). She'll whine, "Mom, I'm bored," when she doesn't want to put away her toys or finish a puzzle. She confuses responsibility with boredom. We all know that being responsible can be very boring indeed, but as adults we don't confuse the concepts.

Our problem is not knowing how to handle "nothing" time. How often do you sit aimlessly flipping channels on your television set wishing something "good" was on? Instead of turning it off, you'll sit there being bored.

You're probably tired. Sitting still is fine, but there's lots to do even then. Listen to music, sew, read a book, meditate, do your photograph albums. Downtime is precious. What you call boredom is a gift of undefined time.

RE-BELIEF: BOREDOM IS CREATIVE

❧Boredom isn't real. Boredom is time that hasn't been filled in by some predetermined commitment or other people's demands. Boredom is lucky. It's the most velvety cushion of simplicity and life—and don't you forget it.

Boredom is stillness, empty space. It's there for you to notice yourself, to take stock of yourself, even to muse aimlessly or daydream. Don't fill it in, don't complain about it, and don't misinterpret it as discontent. It is exceptional creative time and space that allows you to just breathe and not have to account for yourself.

Besides, you don't want to arrive at the end of your life and regret the time you wasted.

Is There a Future for Your Past?

Here it is, in a nutshell:

❧*Learn from the past and discard the regrets.*

Painful, isn't it? You already know this. Living with regret—the great what-if in life—is just a way to prevent you from enjoying your future. Let it go. What is past is really past. Your future will be more productive if you work on forgiveness (forgiving yourself and others), understand, if you can, how or why things might have happened as they did, and then move on to better days.

Obviously, if your past actions have hurt others deeply or caused accidents or even death (such as drunk driving), it's not that easy. But if you don't forgive yourself, you won't be able to know how much better you can be. Maintaining regret is an excuse to fail at the rest of your life.

You can also torment yourself with questions that can't be answered:

Time

What if you had had more understanding parents?
What if you had finished your degree?
What if you hadn't gotten into that car?

These what-ifs are just a way for you to punish yourself for circumstances or poor choices, and since what-if-ing is just another
waste of time, you're making matters worse.

The way to heal is to learn and grow from any experience that
has caused you regret. That is how you evolve.

Let go of the past. You don't have to forget it, but you can—and
should—forgive it. You have a future with hope, opportunity,
potential, in front of you; don't blow it.

Worry It Forward

As for that other what-if—the disease of projecting into the
future—it is just as unproductive.

Once in a while we all succumb to a future-pointed what-if.
What if the market crashes? What if I lose my job? What if my
husband leaves me? What if the sky is falling?

Posing those questions and trying to answer them is a little
game called *fear*. Sure, you can be afraid of the future—in some
ways we all are (after all, we know that one day will be our last).
But it's not a good use of your time to sit now, in your present, and
worry about what might happen. Chances are, no matter how
many scenarios you play out in your worried brain, you won't be
right.

Your future is no more than your next breath.

Your next breath is the only future you really need. Maybe you
need to know who will pick up your children from camp. Maybe
you need to know that there's still a supermarket open after 7 P.M.
when you're on your way home. These are not survival must-
knows. These are the little whispers your inner voice likes to

throw out when you have a moment. It's your inner voice's way of keeping you on your toes—and most often a little thing like "What if I run out of gas?" is a good way to make sure you don't. Those what-ifs aren't what I'm talking about. I'm talking about looking at your child and running through the zillion ways he or she could get hurt. You can worry yourself into apoplexy and it won't prevent a thing.

Another way to play the "future game" is to ponder things that you might like to know, such as will you be successful? Happy? Healthy? But you can't know the answers because you haven't lived your life yet.

Anticipating the future through wandering aimlessly in the land of what-ifs only robs you of what you do have: the present.

People who cling to the past or worry far into the future aren't around much. And they are typically discontent, either reliving unpleasant times or anticipating new painful situations. You will elevate any discontent you have by living outside your normal time zone—which is *now*.

Now's the Time

You'd have to live in an isolation tank not to have heard the phrases (embraced with gusto by New Agers) "Live in the now" and "Be in the moment." Don't get me wrong, they're absolutely right, but how often can you really do that?

It's easy to be in a moment when you're having a good time. Easy, that is, until you start to think that this good time is going to end. Then you start to think about good-byes, endings, next times.

Then there's pain. When you're having a bad time, all you want to do is go to the future of better times. You just wish that your pain would leave. In seminars I attended about death and dying, one speaker talked about being with pain, befriending pain, sitting with pain, making peace with pain, and not resisting it, which causes suffering. He had a point, but isn't that easier said than done?

In stretches of your life where pain is visiting and you just don't like your "now," do your best to tolerate what you have. It's hard to make pain your friend, and frankly, I don't believe that anyone really welcomes pain and sits with it like an old army buddy. Pain stinks. But it is an inevitable part of life. Have someone close to you hold the faith that your life will improve, that your pain will ease. Let yourself believe that your "now" is always changing. That way you know that your pain is going to shift.

RE-BELIEF: THE TIME IS NOW

Your present, not your past, shapes your future.
☙ Your "now" asks you to make choices every moment, and those choices create your future. Choose to act with consciousness and intention. Don't let your life just happen. Choose to be responsible for yourself with everything you do. Your future will turn in the right direction if your intention comes from your heart.

Time will wobble along whether or not you appreciate what you have right this very second. So you might as well walk alongside time rather than running ahead of it or dragging behind. We're all headed to the same place one way or another.

Aging

We're already agreed time accelerates with age. Certainly, the clock can tick slowly if you're alone or ailing and very, very old, but in most cases, time flies with advancing years.

In my twenties, the aging baby boomers overwhelmed me. I'm supposed to be part of this huge population bubble—at the very end of it, according to demographers. I would read about people in their thirties and forties facing aging. I never knew what they were talking about. They sounded so old. I had little patience or sympathy for older boomers. After all, they rented all the good apartments in New York before I was out of college; they became my bosses and drove up the price of real estate before I ever had a chance. I got their crumbs.

Now I'm grateful to this great population. They've all had to face their wrinkles before I did. Those who didn't like these natural creases figured out ways to get rid of them. They've also worked hard to make this country strong. They're also older than I am and always will be. They've made being forty young; even fifty and sixty are young. I'm thinking that ninety is actually when you get to say you're old, but the boomers may change that, too.

If you're young, you won't understand this. If you're older, and I put that at approaching forty and over, you'll know exactly what I'm talking about. Age is so relative. You can be fifty and feel thirty (and act twenty-two). You can be forty-five and look sixty, which is another symptom of stress and discontent. Age can cause a lot of discontent when you care about the number. Take your pick. I've known people to freak out at twenty-five, twenty-six, thirty, thirty-five, forty, and so on. Marking time is a deeply ingrained habit in our culture, and even having an "age crisis" is pretty much acceptable. But it won't change that age is natural and impossible to resist.

RE-BELIEF: AGING

Age is not an enemy, but a friend of contentment.
✍ Here's your bonus: the older you get, the more opportunities you have for finding contentment and for dissolving discontent. I don't mean that you won't have bad days or challenging circumstances, but all that experience you have collected over the years will show you how to cope.

One of the greatest pleasures of aging is being able to speak my mind, my truth, without apology. I can own my own mind, my own opinions, without needing everyone to agree with me. I noticed that the older my friends are, the more fun they have because they don't worry about what other people think of them. You don't like it? Lump it. It's not a dare, but a real, sturdy knowledge in one's beliefs.
You don't have to like what everyone wants you to like.
You don't have to be somewhere you don't want to be.
You don't have to be nice for the sake of being nice (although I believe that common courtesy is important at all ages).

Time

Age absolutely has its blessings. Every year that goes by gives you more opportunity to be your real self. You can live the life you really want. Your children can grow up and find their own lives and give you back time to yourself. Age brings a richness to life; it is not a diminishing factor. Age brings knowledge, experience, courage, calm, patience, and, if you've really worked with your discontent, serenity.

That's not to say that you should allow yourself to go to seed. You can have all that wisdom and still keep up the appearance you like. (I won't take a stand on elective surgeries, but *be careful* if you go that route.) I like to think that you can take some easy, noninvasive steps for your appearance and not look as if you're trying to deny your age. But I haven't been there yet myself.

Be aware, though, that nothing makes you look older than a bad hairpiece or bad dye job, too much makeup or too youthful clothes. Be reasonable about what you expect to look like as you get older or you're going to have to read the "Self-Esteem" chapter again.

Age brings you exploration, new interests, and more time for current interests, hobbies, even new careers. Age gives you more time to explore your karma and to give back to those who have given to you. Age brings perspective and the opportunity to pass along wisdom to future generations. Age gives time. And that's what this is all about.

Anger

ALTHOUGH anger can be found in almost every topic—and in every section this book covers—I feel it deserves its own place in a book about discontent.

A whole lot of anger is going on in our world, and some of it is inside you. Anger is not itself a cause of discontent, but keeping anger inside certainly is. Since most of us have grown up in a "Have a nice day" society, we haven't been taught to deal with anger effectively. Smile, suck it up, and move on. Turn the other cheek. Let it go—but the reality is, you can't.

Were You Expecting Something?

Anger is simply the reaction you have when your expectations are not met. You think you should win first place in your tennis tournament. You don't. You're angry. You think you should meet the love of your life. You don't. You're frustrated and angry. You think you're next in line for promotion. You're not. You're feeling overlooked, angry, and frightened. What if you're never going to be promoted? You might also feel rejected or hurt in some of these circumstances, but when you move out of that phase, you'll find your anger; it's healing. Actually, it's healing if you let it out. If you don't, you're begging for discontent.

Anything can make you angry. You don't have to justify being angry—you just are. This is where many of us veer off course. How many times have you tried to reason yourself out of being angry? Ever hear this kind of reaction?

"I shouldn't be angry because he didn't mean it."

"Don't be angry—it was an accident."

189

"I shouldn't be angry because it's not their fault if they can't help me."

Guess what?

You can be angry. Go for it.

Jump up and down and scream and kick if you like. The more you deny that anger, the more it builds up. Take action and relieve the pressure, because the more it builds up, the more likely it is that you'll blow up at something silly, just to get it out. You'll be a walking belching volcano about to blow. Don't go postal, baby. You can prevent it.

If you find yourself getting angry or irritated quickly, you're storing up too much anger. Say you get home from the grocery store and you find that one egg among the dozen you just bought is broken. You lose it. You're furious. You can't get back to the store for a million reasons, and even if you could, is it worth that much time just to get one egg? Honey, you have some big anger stored up in there. If something little sets you off, you're probably overstuffed with unexpressed anger.

Behind the Scene

Behind anger is something common, pervasive, and hard to face: fear. Half the time people get angry, it's a fear reaction. Now I do say only *half* the time because I know that you can get genuinely pissed off about things in life. Yet you should be aware that a lot of that anger you've experienced—or are experiencing—is coming from fear.

Fear of being abandoned, taken advantage of, fear of humiliation, fear of being unemployable, unlovable, unacceptable, imperfect. Rejection can be hard to take—personally, I loathe it—but it's a reality. No life is without rejection. Sometimes being rejected can be a gift, a way of redirecting you into a better direction.

Examine your anger and recognize what is really unmet expectation and what is simply fear. You'll notice that sometimes the two are so close together, it's hard to tell.

Don't Boil, Melt

Everyone has a boiling point where anger erupts like volcanic activity. Everyone also has a melting point, a less known, more neglected internal release valve. The melting point releases the pressure of the building anger without force. It lends perspective to the situation and allows you an out.

PRELIMINARY ANGER INSTRUCTIONS:
FIND YOUR MELTING POINT

☙ Your melting point is the place where you can momentarily remove yourself from the anger-inducing circumstances and see the bigger picture. It's a moment of perspective that replaces rigid rage with a sigh of understanding. Every day we have opportunities to melt instead of stiffen or focus on the single offense that incited our anger. Once you master an essential melting point, your anger can be reduced, relaxed, or diffused. You won't have to have a heart attack due to keeping your anger inside.

Anger's Playgrounds

Daily life presents us with many delightful opportunities to test our melting points. Here are a few circumstances in which we've all experienced anger.

Poor Customer Service

Once upon a time, you would walk into a store, be greeted by a clerk who cared about helping you. You wouldn't feel pressured to buy anything, but you would be able to view and discuss options for whatever you wanted to purchase. It was a simpler time. There were no catalogs except for Sears'. There were no 800 numbers or

Web sites. You couldn't find a store open on a Sunday. People cared about your business and wanted you to come back.

We have a lot of convenience now. We can buy virtually anything within minutes of wanting it. We can avoid human contact altogether (if we want to). But we've lost a lot of respect for the process of buying and selling. We're in a hurry. We expect instant gratification. We expect common courtesy—and all of this expectation can land us deep into frustration and eventually add to our anger and discontent.

We've all been there.

There are so many reasons to be angry with what is loosely called "customer service" or "customer relations." Personally I find it hard to live with long voice menus, punching in endless account numbers and security codes, waiting on hold for a human voice, finding that human voice unable to help or uninterested in what I need to accomplish, and worse, finding that all my effort went nowhere because someone didn't care enough to do his job. Conducting almost any business transaction—banking, making airline or restaurant reservations—can strike a match to your fuse. It's okay to be angry about the way people treat you in impersonal situations.

Ultimately you want to be heard. You want to be noticed. You want your needs to matter. When your needs are not met, you get angry. And you have a right to be.

Getting angry at bad customer service is useless. You will get hung up on if you yell on the phone. You will be hauled off by security if you raise your voice at an airport. You can be rendered so helpless and angry that you might do something really stupid.

My husband has what I call bad travel karma. He regularly ends up on flights that are nine hours late, once from a transatlantic carrier's complete toilet malfunction, or because the air traffic control tower has lost power. All true—and it rubs off on us when we travel together. As you'd expect, he gets really angry. I calm him down by composing our letter to the customer service department of the airline in question. It's fun to do because we can write all sorts of awful things, which I edit before it is sent. We almost always get a written acknowledgment and some sort of make-up offer. Now, we're just resigned to always having bad travel experiences. An uneventful trip, to us, is a cause for wonder and awe.

MELTING POINT INSTRUCTIONS
FOR POOR CUSTOMER SERVICE

- ❧Get it out (a letter is effective), then find perspective: you're not at their mercy forever.
- *Take your business elsewhere next time.*
  ❧Report your experience to that company and to the Better Business Bureau and to your state commerce authorities. You do have power, and exercising it will help dissolve your anger.
- *Use the Internet.*
  ❧Cyberspace offers a wealth of shared experience. You can find a community that shares its clout and expertise to make your complaints heard effectively.
- *Remain calm.*
  ❧Calm, organized complaints get more attention than screaming hysterics. You won't be alone in your anger, and simply finding others in the same boat can make you feel better.

Standing in Line

This is related to customer service. Waiting is not something anyone likes to do. If you're waiting for test results—be they academic or medical—the wait can be excruciating. If you're waiting in line for the cashier at the grocery store, or at the post office, you get frustrated. Waiting in too many places in a single day can become a great source of anger and discontent. Even when you live in the now and you allow your time to be fluid, you can still get angry when your time is wasted by waiting.

I think the worst situation is when someone skips ahead of you after you've been patiently waiting. I watched a woman jump a line at a train station because her train was going to leave in four minutes, while the lady in front of me who had waited quietly and politely for her turn was trying to make the same train—and missed it.

Recently I was trying to have lunch with a friend at a local restaurant. It's a popular lunch place and we put our names down along with everyone around us. We watched three pairs of people waltz in from the street and get seated without any waiting at all, while thirty minutes later my blood sugar was so low I felt faint. I made a minor scene with the staff, who couldn't have cared less and denied (lied!) seating anyone out of order. When I finally got seated, I allowed myself to eat lunch there for the last time. I won't give that place one more nickel of my hard-earned money. Where I go and where I spend my money is my choice, and I don't give it away lightly. Nor should you.

Gossip columnists love to cite instances where celebrities make a scene when they aren't automatically skipped over lines for a bathroom or allowed first into a party—considering themselves better or more important than everyone else waiting. It just adds to the rage. Do you think cancer researchers are allowed to skip to the front? Or great humanitarians or philanthropists? Nope. Kind of makes you mad.

What do you do with all that anger?

MELTING POINT INSTRUCTIONS FOR WAITING

- *You have a choice—and power to exercise it.*

  ❧Unless you're standing in line for something you legally need or have to do, such as acquiring a visa stamp on your passport or a driver's license renewal, or are at a security checkpoint, you can leave. Once you take back your power and understand that it's your choice to stand in line and not an obligation imposed on you by someone else, your patience can return. Breathe. Think about a nice memory. Think about something you can make for dinner. Do butt-tightening exercises. Daydream. Use the time as creative space. If you're running late as a result of this line, borrow a cell phone or run and make a phone call so that you won't inconvenience the other people in your life.

194

Anger

- **Respect your choice to stay or go.**

   ❧Make your decision and live with it—no second-guessing. Is your time worth standing in line? Is waiting for your McDonald's meal worth being late for work? Is waiting to pay your phone bill better than buying a stamp (unless, of course, there's a huge line at the post office)? What is worth it? You can answer that question for yourself, then accept your choice. Exercise your free will. It's not hard and you don't have to sweat it.

Bad Manners

It's hard to understand why people don't bother with manners when a simple word or two can make all the difference. Bad manners are the root of many of the previous anger-producing, discontent-raising situations.

Poor customer service? Often it's caused by bad manners.

Line jumpers? Rude people.

Road rage? Just what did that hand signal mean, anyway?

How heavy your discontent feels can be related to how you handle situations of stress. Not only are the previous Instructions helpful, but a little common courtesy can go a long way, too.

When in doubt, act politely. It's not a terribly hard rule to learn and live by, but it does seem to be fading from our society.

I live on a fairly congested street. Often, people are milling around, taking up space on the sidewalk and not very interested in getting out of the way. I once walked through a crowd of young, loud girls and kept saying "Pardon me" without the slightest result. I couldn't take a step without someone in the way. Common courtesy would suggest that the group stand aside so that pedestrians could get by. I accidentally bumped into a girl and said, "Excuse me," and kept going. She hadn't heard me (or pretended not to) and turned to me screaming, "Don't you disrespect me, you bitch! I don't disrespect you. You don't disrepect me!"

I turned to give her a puzzled look and she took the opportunity to wave her finger in my face and scream more fury at me. When she stopped for a breath, I responded, "I said, 'Excuse me,' but you

195

didn't hear me because you were talking. And, just for the record, screaming and waving your finger is not going to earn you my respect."

I turned and walked away. She was still screaming at me. Her posse wasn't too happy with me either.

I felt like an ancient grandmother prevailing upon her granddaughter to comport herself with dignity. Manners seem to have gone out of fashion. It is a great pity, because if we employed common courtesies, a lot less anger would be going around. Children taught good manners feel comfortable in new situations and carry this ease all through life. They automatically fall back on courteous, diplomatic behavior, which gives them an advantage whatever they encounter.

MELTING POINT INSTRUCTIONS IN THE FACE OF BAD MANNERS

- *Be an example.*
  ✍Conducting yourself with poise, dignity, and manners is always a winning formula. The more you show the world how well good manners work, the more the world will use them.
- *Remember the rules of karma.*
  ✍Your karma will improve if you conduct yourself with compassion, and though you may enjoy only a few moments of superiority for taking that high road, you will not regret it. Those whose bad manners have made you uncomfortable will have to live with their mistakes.

Traffic

Road rage is now an accepted form of social deviance around the world. That's frightening.

Everyone seems to be going somewhere in a hurry, and with a sense of self-importance and entitlement. That's the perfect recipe for road rage. It makes me angry at the automobile industry and the irresponsibility of cities without efficient public transportation.

Anger

I've never owned a car, but I've had my share of anger in traffic. I'm married to the most traffic-intolerant person on the planet (no doubt tied to his appalling travel karma). Traffic is certainly a trigger for his and others' anger. You're trying to get somewhere and traffic is there to prevent you from doing it. You can do nothing about traffic other than to stay where you are or try a different route, mode of transportation, or time of day. You are bound to run into traffic—air traffic, street traffic, even foot traffic. I got angry with the traffic in swimming pool lanes when I wanted to do laps.

At times, someone or something is going to get in your way. That's the reality of living in our world. It's how *you* handle it that makes a difference.

The Dalai Lama went to Los Angeles not long ago and was said to have blessed the traffic there for giving him more time to meditate. It works for me when I'm in a taxi and the traffic is bumper-to-bumper. Sitting in unmoving traffic or being a passenger is a must, however. You can't meditate behind the wheel even at twenty miles an hour. I suggest books on tape for that.

However practical my advice may be, the meaning of traffic and its impact on you goes deeper. Why are you intolerant of waiting? What is your hurry?

You can ask yourself a lot of questions before you get angry and even bypass anger if you're willing to be honest with yourself. Few people can claim a life-or-death reason for getting out of a traffic jam.

MELTING POINT INSTRUCTIONS FOR TRAFFIC

- *Breathe through your anger and frustration.*
  ❧No amount of screaming or honking is going to make things move any faster. The only place you'll get with road rage is in the hospital—with high blood pressure, heart disease, or something worse.
- *You are responsible for yourself.*
  ❧Your actions and reactions are your domain. Choose the "high road" and act as an example for your children and in a way that you can be proud of.

Until public transportation is more pervasive or gas prices climb too high, traffic is a way of life in our culture. It's not personal.

Computers

I never knew how fast my temper could rise until I started working on a computer. Ever lose your work because of a crash or a mishit button? Ever have to keep restarting your computer because it just won't work? Ever have to wade through manuals and voice-messaging systems to get some help? (Back to customer service.)

At my computer store, where I have unloaded my share of discontent, I asked my friend George about my hypothesis: computers bring out anger faster than any other piece of technology. He enlightened me with his take on computer discontent:

"You develop a relationship with your computer. Even if it's just for work, it has what you need on it. It's your friend. If you don't have access to it or it doesn't talk to you when you need it, it makes you crazy. My motorcycle, my only mode of transportation, is in the shop right now and I don't even mind. If it were my computer, I'd be nuts."

We do develop a relationship with our computer—and our cell phone and all other electronic must-haves. We develop a dependence and a reliance that are probably a tad unhealthy. It's what codependence was in the nineties—we now have tech dependence, and it can make us neurotic.

It doesn't help that we don't understand how our computers work and that there isn't a quick alternative if they go on the blink (unlike when cell phones break, there's always the old-fashioned land line). A computer is a mysterious maze of chips, wires, and components encased in plastic. It communicates in complex languages that break down into a series of 0's and 1's. I had to learn to write an algorithm (a computer-science command sequence) when I was in college. It was really hard to wrap my mind around a new way of thinking. Of course, once you understand how computers work, it's more interesting, but it doesn't guarantee you'll actually enjoy them. In college I learned a computer language called FOR-TRAN, which is now extinct, but my lightweight exposure to computer languages does not translate into any kind of computer savvy now. My computer holds all my books, ideas, correspondence, astrological charts, and a whole lot of other stuff, and I am at its mercy.

MELTING POINT INSTRUCTIONS FOR COMPUTER RAGE

- *Take a break.*
  ❧Embrace the gift of free time when your computer goes to the hospital. You are not going to be annihilated—you will survive—without a computer for a few days. If you're desperate for e-mail, go to a cybercafé.
- *Save your work.*

Admittedly, I haven't yet mastered any true peace with the snafus and troubles I've encountered. I know intellectually that I will be fine without a computer, but it hits me on a survival level because it is where I work. As a result, I take care of myself. I have a backup laptop just in case. (Full disclosure: After I wrote this, I backed it up on a Zip disk.)

Not everyone will be prone to computer rage. Yet you aren't alone if you find yourself smashing your mouse, hitting your keyboard, or swearing at the longest download in history. Computers live in the realm of electronic energy (in astrology they are ruled by Uranus, the planet of eccentricity), and it is not a stable or safe place. You'll be disappointed if you think any electronic device is going to be consistent and "there" for you.

Justifiable, Undeniable Anger

While it is important to be aware of those everyday irritations and provocations that can push you to your boiling point, life sometimes hands us really impossible situations that aren't simple to release. They feel personal and awful.

Instructions for Your Discontent

In some circumstances in your life you have no voice or power, and you feel the victim of injustice. Maybe a teacher didn't give you a passing grade but you know you deserved one. Or you didn't get a promotion and complaining is only going to look like sour grapes. It's highly likely that the world is going to treat you unfairly one day. I used to work for a misanthrope whose favorite expression was *"Fair* is a one-word oxymoron."

I have no explanation for why all of us suffer from injustices. I know only that whatever anger you have about it needs to be released, or you will be a prisoner to that injustice the rest of your life. That wound will rule you. And that's really not fair.

The anger born out of injustice is difficult to release because in most cases you won't have immediate recourse; you might feel silenced. Once an injustice is rendered, it's hard to make everything all right with a simple apology—if you can get one. Most often, your anger rests in many levels of your consciousness but is almost silent. If you feel powerless to express yourself, you'll only become angrier. It's not enough to say "I'm angry." You have to feel it, act on it, release it. Once that anger is gone, you're a step closer to forgiveness, the great healer.

I give this anger-releasing recipe out regularly. It really works and you don't have to confront the source of the conflict to cope. If you're passive-aggressive, this is a way to vent your anger without beginning that cycle of emotional destruction.

INSTRUCTIONS FOR RELEASING DEEP ANGER

❧ Releasing anger is a four-part process:
- *Speak*
- *Feel*
- *Act*
- *Release*

  ❧ This means you have to acknowledge it aloud, allow emotions to surface, and be able to physically shake out your anger. Releasing anger is more about handing it over to another place, diffusing it so that you don't have it sitting in your heart for the rest of your life. Since I have no problem getting angry, I'm an expert. Many of my clients are the opposite: they don't like to even acknowledge their anger, let alone act on it.

Step 1: Speak

- *Claim it.*

   ☙ This is the first step: the ability to admit you're angry. You can do this alone or with someone else. I didn't know it was all right to be angry until I was twenty-five. I had been walking around with a huge storm cloud over my head for years. My parents called me Chief Thundercloud because I was in a bad mood so often. I didn't realize that I had unspent anger—justified or not—and that I needed to release it. When someone told me that it was okay to get pissed off—even if my inner voice told me I shouldn't get mad—I relaxed. It's easier to be angry and release it than to pretend you're not angry and swallow it.

- *It's all in the acknowledgment, not in the volume.*

   ☙ If you like, you can yell or scream "I'm angry!" like a child. "I'm mad as hell and I'm not going to take it anymore!" Or you can simply sigh and say, "Yep, I'm angry."

Step 2: Feel

- *Access your anger so that you can feel your body respond to it.*

   ☙ Often, speaking and feeling the anger go hand in hand so you'll feel it when you acknowledge it. Are you stiff? Are you aching to hit something? Are you energetic? Anger is like a geyser; it roars when released. Keeping it packed down in your body is like squashing a power source. Feel the anger in you and you will be able to act with it.

Step 3: Act

- *Do something with your anger.*

   ☙ I like to kickbox. You might want to hit a pillow. You can run, jog, play basketball—whatever you feel like doing. Anger needs to be expressed physically, and just thinking about the source of your anger and channeling that energy into your squash game can improve your athletic results as well as relieve you of some of that pressure. Anger is such a wonderful current of unexpressed energy that if we could only channel it into fuel, we'd never have a gas shortage.

- *A burst of anger can break inertia in any part of your life.*

❧Have you ever updated your résumé when you got really angry at work? You can use your anger to do something productive—even just cleaning closets or getting your garden weeded. There's so much therapy out there for angry hands. Just take a look and set to a chore as an act to let out your anger. I can run a whole extra mile when I'm really mad.

Step 4: Release
- *Let it go when you feel spent.*

❧You can do this in a few different ways. You can simply say "I'm over it" or "I surrender" and you'll be able to feel the truth of that statement. You can feel yourself relax and you won't cringe or wince whenever you think about the source of your anger.

My favorite method of release is burning paper. I just write down what has been bugging me on a piece of paper and burn it in my kitchen sink (so that nothing else will catch on fire). Using fire is cleansing—fire is a purifier and a transformer; it reduces things to ash. I use its elemental power to burn the source of my anger symbolically. It is a nice, final form of release and usually works well.

- *Be warned, however, that even though you say you've released your anger, you'll probably have to revisit that issue.*

❧Once you think you're clear of it, someone will bring it up—in conversation or in an e-mail or in an unexpected way. It's as if the universe is testing you to see if you're really over it or if you were just kidding yourself. Being beyond anger doesn't mean that you won't react to it anymore. I still get steamed up—briefly—about things that happened to me fifteen years ago. Why shouldn't I? If it made me angry then, it would probably make me angry today—but I don't hang on to it. The whole point of the release is to make sure you're not walking around with unexpressed anger and to make sure you don't sabotage yourself with a long-held grudge. Life is full of disappointments, so releasing anger is a lifelong process.

Grudges and Discontent

Grudges are solid, sour, dense wounds that anchor anger and hurt, a real downer. I come from a long line of grudge holders. My father used to say that he held hereditary grudges from his grandfather and didn't even know why.

Grudges seem pretty useful in everyday life. They keep you from doing business with or making friends with "bad" people. They keep you from being taken advantage of. They are also effective in anchoring distrust, suspicion, and negativity. You don't have to love everyone or even make peace with someone who has done you wrong, but you might want to let some grudges go as time passes.

I'm not one to deny you a good grudge or two, but be careful not to harbor too many dusty old hurts, because they can add up and get heavy. Who wants to haul around a huge bag of grudges? You think it's protecting you, and to some extent it is, but is it worth the drag? Think about a grudge you're holding right now. Doesn't it bring up anger, distrust, discomfort? Doesn't a dark cloud surround you when you remember why you're holding this grudge? It certainly does. When you think about it, why would you let this person cause you even more pain? That's what's happening. Your grudge is holding on to that irksome hurt; you have to experience it again and again. That is not a good thing.

I suggest a periodic grudge review. Stay away from people you don't like, but don't hold on to whatever past hurt they caused you. I'd say a grudge is worth about a year, two at the most. If you can't get past something after two years, you have some serious forgiveness work to do. You're probably angrier with yourself than you are with the person who caused you pain in the first place.

We talked about forgiveness in family relationships, and now is the time to apply it to yourself. Most of us harbor untapped anger and grudges that we bury and keep for future use because we want to remind ourselves how we screwed up. It's that negative inner voice, that self-esteem issue we've already addressed.

"Don't you remember how that guy took advantage of you? You have to *hate* him!"

What that voice is saying is "You idiot, you put yourself in his way and he took you for a fool. You *are* a fool, aren't you?"

That voice is making you hold a grudge; it might even push you to hate someone. It's saying that you took a chance on someone and didn't come through and you have to be punished for it.

I'm here to tell you that you don't have to be punished. Giving someone a chance to prove worthy of your trust is not a stupid thing. Hopefully you thought this person wouldn't let you down. If you had possessed perfect information and known beforehand that this person was not going to come through for you, would you have been trusting? No, not unless you're a masochist.

You can't blame yourself for mistakes that others make. You can be angry, sure; you can review and learn from the situation so that it won't happen again—or at least you can try to prevent it from happening again. But you have to forgive yourself for giving someone a chance to come through for you. Big deal. If you lost money, it will probably come back to you (but watch that grudge energy because negativity hinders prosperity). If you were deceived, that bad karma isn't going to be your karma in the future—it goes to the deceiver. You can and should rely on karmic justice to work out the issues of wrongdoings.

My latest grudge has to do with a friend of mine (now an ex-friend) who over the years took advantage of my helper mentality as long as I was needed, only to cut me off rudely when I was no longer necessary. I cannot tell you what a chump I was. This is probably the third or fourth time this has happened, and I've decided it will be the last. I used to be one of those suckers who is always there for someone in pain. I can't resist the urge to help someone if she needs it (only if she asks, though—I've learned the hard way about that). So I was there for an old friend who sustained a sad family crisis. I spoke on the phone with her (she lived far away) every day for about eighteen months. When it was clear that the healing was over and her moment of need had passed, she was rude to me. I hung up the phone that day thinking it was just a weird moment. I called her back twice, left a message, and never received a response. I've been fuming, *fuming*—with steam coming out of my ears—for a month. It's time to let it go. I don't have to give her one more morsel of my energy and I'm not going to.

So here's how I'm going to do it. It's all about forgiving myself. This is going to sound familiar. It is similar to the family forgiveness meditation in the section on relationships. The difference here is that you have to face yourself.

INSTRUCTIONS FOR DISSOLVING GRUDGES

✿ Define a time and space where you can be alone, undisturbed, and free to relax. No phones, TV, e-mail, pager, cell phone—*nothing* to distract you. Find a comfortable position and close your eyes. Breathe, unhurriedly and deeply, so that you feel your body relax more and more. With each breath, feel calm spaciousness around you. Nothing feels tight, close, heavy, or anxious. Even thinking about the person who gets to you most is all right. You can handle it.

When you're ready, in your mind's eye, picture yourself standing in a serene setting. In the distance you can see someone approaching you. This person walks slowly and purposefully toward you, and as you watch, you see that this person is you. You watch yourself stop. You look into your own eyes. You see your own power. You appreciate your own body.

Reach out and embrace this person, this you. Say aloud, "I forgive you."

Let it happen. Be with yourself in this meditation as long as you need to be. You are healing self-inflicted wounds. You are embracing your vulnerability and your power.

The first time I tried a similar forgiveness meditation for a another emotional wound that hadn't healed, I burst into tears. I didn't know that I had stored so many reservations and judgments about myself. I hadn't really felt it until I did this powerful meditation.

When you let yourself off the hook for all the boo-boos, missteps, and bad judgment calls that you've made in your life, you immediately experience an overwhelming sense of compassion and relief. It is emotionally exhausting but ultimately freeing and relaxing. Your demons, grudges, angers, and wounds are reduced and often healed so much that you can go about life more optimistically than ever before.

Forgiving yourself as an adult can bring back that wide-open hopefulness and energy you had as a child, before the world got so complicated.

Spiritual Discontent

Existential Discontent

SPIRITUAL discontent finds its way into our lives most often through the newspaper, on the television, and by word of mouth. It's close to the surface of consciousness but never an overriding concern except in special circumstances. We live with spiritual discontent constantly: the shattering terrorist attack on the World Trade Center; photos and stories about starving children in faraway places; the horrors invoked by hostile, dictatorial regimes; people being abducted, tortured, and murdered; ferocious disease devastating entire populations. Had enough? There's always more.

How can you handle all of this? After a while, you can't take the horrors of these realities. What can you do about it? Is it enough to give money to the Red Cross? To Amnesty International? What is enough? Should I assist Doctors Without Borders or become a Peace Corps volunteer? I can't save the world, make a living (and make dinner), and be a good mother, wife, and citizen. It's too much, I tell you!

Of course it is. The world is full of woes and you aren't expected to solve them all. You don't even have to solve one. But you can look at your own neighborhood and find a situation where a little compassion, generosity, or support in the way of prayer would be a great gesture for healing. Maybe an elderly woman needs help shopping, or a baby's parents can't afford toys or clothes. There might be a sick child with no hope of a cure whose parents just appreciate your thoughts. That's a great start.

But your spiritual discontent is only going to be partially resolved by keeping your own corner of the world in your heart. Your newspaper, radio, or television is going to shovel another pile of world woes at your feet. You'll see stories about famine in

Africa, prostitution and white slavery in Eastern Europe, and even the self-serving white-collar crime in our own country that you (we) will end up paying for. There's no end to the ills of the world.

This is your spiritual discontent. This is your soul and your heart reacting to something that is desperately wrong. It's going to happen again and again because we live in an imperfect world. How can we all deal with it?

INSTRUCTIONS FOR SPIRITUAL DISCONTENT, PART I

Give your power a voice.
✤ The power of acknowledgment is the first step toward healing your sense of helplessness. Don't be afraid to talk about what bothers you. Point it out to others. Raise consciousness. It doesn't matter whom you talk to, but writing to your mayor, a city council member, a senator, or a congressman is not a bad idea. Use the Internet if you're pressed for time. There's no harm in voicing your opinion. It is your right in a free country and your best use of your free will. Let someone know that you care. Your voice joins others. Many voices make a great sound. Sound is energy. Energy is work. You never know what you might accomplish just by saying "I care."

Understandably, your caring doesn't have to mean "I'll go there and work on it." Acknowledgment means that you see what is happening. You aren't turning your back on something painful and you register what is happening. Even if you cannot take action, acknowledgment is better than pretending it's not there at all. Don't deny it, because that's dangerous. Denial is permission to let it go on. Denial or turning your eyes away and pretending not to see something unpleasant is being complicit. It makes you part of the crime.

During the Reagan era, dramatic cuts in government spending released onto our city streets a substantial population of people who didn't "fit" into normal society. Between war-rattled Vietnam veterans and socially dysfunctional or mentally impaired adults, our streets soon filled with homeless people. Some of them were drunks or drug addicts; some were schizophrenic. Some were just the victims of circumstance.

Homelessness was a huge issue at the time. There was outrage from people who demanded the government take more responsibility, and outrage from those who just didn't want their streets full of indigents. As a result, institutions and organizations that deal directly with homeless people sprang up, but homelessness is still a problem for which there is no easy solution.

During those early days when homelessness was a relatively new phenomenon, I didn't know what my response should be. Sometimes I gave money to panhandlers, sometimes I bought them food (this was almost always refused), sometimes I just rolled my eyes, sickened by what I smelled and saw. I felt guilty and helpless. I wanted to find a way to help that wasn't prompted by obligation or guilt. Then someone told me that the answer was simply to acknowledge them. If I was asked for money and I wanted to give it, I had to look that homeless person in the eye. Make it personal. This was a person, not an animal. It was a lot harder than just handing over a dollar while walking quickly by. Look into their eyes. See that they exist. They will know that you acknowledge them. It sounds so simple, but it's much more complex.

INSTRUCTIONS FOR SPIRITUAL DISCONTENT,
PART II

Allow yourself to acknowledge the bad things in the world.
❧ Find a place in yourself that allows acknowledgment. Balance compassion and dispassion and you will not feel guilt. Be a witness to your world.

There is a reason for everything. If you believe in God, you know that spirit works from mystery. We can't understand the concept of God, the universe, time, life beyond death. . . . Spirit is based on faith, not fact. Homeless people remind us of how much we have. If you believe in karma, homeless people have, on some karmic level, volunteered for that job and serve to remind us that we cannot take everything we have for granted.

Look for the larger meaning in the world's woes and your spiritual discontent will ease.

Chances are you have a home and you have seen a homeless person. If you get angry at seeing that person, it is only a cover for your fear. If you feel sad, you need to acknowledge that person and offer help if you want to. If you feel "Gosh, I am so blessed to have what I have," that homeless being has touched your spirit and has served God in a mysterious way.

The cows being slaughtered because of mad cow disease highlighted that some cattle were being fed animal matter. Cows are vegetarians, and as a result of this disease, their feed was reviewed.

Like the homeless, children who are born into poverty raise our consciousness of our own riches, health, and prosperity. You are not being prodded to feel guilty, only to be conscious of how much you possess.

Women stripped of their rights and common human dignities are there to reinforce our beliefs in gender equality and to help us hold the faith that, one day, all people will be able to exercise their free will.

Your diffuse spiritual discontent will ease and your life will lighten, not harden, when you acknowledge the darker sides of our world.

Knowledge is power. Power has influence. Influence can make change.

Most of the ills of the earth are similar strokes of God's brush. They can cause diffuse discontent and helplessness. I don't know why God chooses certain creatures to undergo horrors or suffering.

I do know that injustice and cruelty stir us into action and prayer. Both action and prayer make a difference. Action dissolves your discontent when you exercise some part of yourself to say "I want to help." Prayer makes a difference because it asks the universe for healing and compassion.

Sermon

Religion and spirituality are not the same thing. Some people find spirituality in their religion. Some find spirituality outside organized religion. Some never exhibit any spirituality but consider themselves religious. Discontent finds its way into religion and spirituality when you or someone else is convinced that only one belief is right. Once you judge others to be either right or wrong, you are asking for a permanent dose of discontent.

In the West, we are fortunate to have religious freedom, but we are unfortunate not to have religious tolerance guaranteed in our hearts.

Whatever you believe, you are entitled to your opinion. Judge others based on their beliefs and you will soak yourself in discontent. You are setting up a Right and Wrong that you may believe to be the Truth, but it's only your truth.

You can make only your life and your choices correct within the context of your chosen religion or spirituality. You can't tell someone else what to do for the simple reason that you are not God.

All religions are searching for some sense of spiritual leadership and moral structure. Religion is great for that if it works for you. If it doesn't, you can still find your spirit.

Watch out for your judgments about religion and the discontent you cause yourself or others. I don't believe any religion tells you to be better than or righter than anyone else. Can you picture yourself telling God "I killed someone in your name!" or "I've hated on your behalf!" It's as ridiculous as waging war to "keep the peace." That is not an act of spiritual enlightenment. Making judgments about someone's spiritual destiny or taking negative action in the name of God only puts you in a dubious position for your future karma and, if you believe in it, Judgment Day.

Discontent Rewind:
The Deceit of Attainment

One last powerful lesson with discontent comes from attaining contentment. The more you address the core of your discontent, the more often you'll find that calm paradise of contentment. But here's the lesson: it's not permanent.

I have clients and associates who get a nasty shock when they realize that all they have finally achieved—all those hard-won goals—won't make them happy forever. No amount of money, recognition, or success can make you really happy forever. Sure, children and a spouse can fill your heart, but they are not all of you all the time; they're only part of who you are. Having it all—whatever your "all" is—can minimize struggles or smooth over paths, but if you expect permanent happiness or contentment from getting what you want, you're going to be unpleasantly surprised.

❧ *You are here to evolve. Discontent will return.*

Getting what you want can be a discontent in itself. Attainment is frightening because you think you have nowhere to go.

You don't need money. You don't desire any more loving relationships. You have time, you aren't angry, you might even meditate or pray. But you still feel scared or empty. What's going on?

You are constantly evolving and changing. If you think you're done, you're not.

I have a cousin in Hollywood who knows a lot of rich, famous, beautiful people. These people don't ever have to work again. They have satisfying relationships. They work for charity. They have a connection to spirit. They have great homes. Some of them are handling it all just swell, but that's because they still have goals, dreams, and passions to explore. They are evolving, releasing the hold on "having my dreams" to create new dreams, new desires, new passions to fulfill. They still allow discontent its due.

Those who got all they wanted and argued they were "set for life" met with grave results: addiction and depression, and in some cases suicide. They attained the "top" and decided there was no room for further discontent. It takes a lot of artificial stimulants to keep unhappiness at bay.

"Having it all" is not a healthy place to be any more than "having nothing to live for" is. It's the same thing. What is there to live for if you don't allow yourself to learn and grow? What you need is a little scratching discontent to give you a new lesson or purpose to work with. You're not finished yet!

Lighten Up

While you will never be completely rid of discontent, you will become more skillful as it infringes on your life.

Every bit of work you do in alleviating your discontent is going to make you more prepared for the next time it visits.

✆ *Dissolving discontent makes you a lighter spirit.*

With practice, discontent won't hit you so hard nor stay so long. You can handle it without sinking into fear. Your ability to process and work with change evolves with each discontent you encounter. The more change you handle, the less frightening it will become. Using these Instructions makes you more agile and skillful in working through your problems. As each form of discontent recedes, you'll find yourself lighter, more joyful, more accepting, more compassionate, and more fulfilled throughout your life.

✆ *As your fear decreases, your ability to enjoy life increases.*

You will know that you have increased your skills with discontent and its side effects because even in the face of new potholes and problems, your inner core won't be shaken. Deep down, you'll know that you'll be okay, even more than okay, once you've worked it through. You can keep some part of yourself aside from any discontent, and this part of you is calm, trusting, and allowing.

Your Own Instructions

Your Own Instructions

The Final Word

The Delights of Discontent

I DON'T want to leave you with the impression that we have to struggle in order to be happy. These Instructions are meant to minimize the grief of learning experiences, life improvement, and self-improvement.

Discontent is dynamic. It can arrive in great clumps of difficulties or in spiky, minor annoyances. Discontent may not always be center stage in your life, but it will always be there. It finds its way into every life to keep you active and alert, questioning and achieving.

Now you have more perspective on those difficult times. Now you know that a surfacing tension in your life could be just a passing annoyance or a sign of deeper change on its way. The more attention you give to your life, the faster you'll diagnose the roots of your discontent.

These Instructions are not just for reading. Use them. Take action when things get tough. Dare to believe there's a way to learn and grow even from disappointment, pain, or anger. Allow yourself to participate in your life and steer your way through challenging times.

Once you've successfully applied some Instructions, you'll feel more powerful and more alive. You'll see that you do have a voice in your future and that you do have power over your choices. Even better, you'll know that when times get tough again, you'll be able to face them.

Even though discontent isn't easy, it has its advantages. It makes you a better person. It builds you a better life.

Now let's get going.

Index of Instructions
and Re-Beliefs

Index of Instructions and Re-Beliefs

Acknowledgments

Because of the subject matter of this book, I have to thank all the nasty, miserable people and circumstances that have contributed to my discontent.

More important, I particularly want to thank those people who guided me or at least tolerated me through those bad times:

My husband, Gero; daughter, Elisabeth. My family, Randy, Amy, John, Carol and Sean, Mom and Dick, Halo and Friedel.

Friends Alan H., Boris, Cheryl C., Cheryl K., Cindy, Hank, Julia, Liz, Mandy, Mary Lou, Mitch, Nancy1, Nancy2, Rachel, Shaye, Sheila, Shelly, Susan, and Tiffany T.

My friends from way back, Beth, Biff, Jane, Judith, Judy, Kayo, Margaret, and Margie.

My agent, Emma Sweeney, and editors Jake Morrissey and Brenda Copeland.

And, of course, magical Sarah Ban B!

About the Author

Barrie Dolnick is the author of several books, including *Sexual Bewitchery* and *How to Write a Love Letter.* She is also a high-profile consultant whose company, Executive Mystic Services, uses alternative information techniques, including tarot cards, astrology, mediation, and spell casting to guide clients to fulfill their potential. She lives in New York City with her husband and daughter. Visit her Web site at www.barriedolnick.com